Francis Frith's

Devon Churches

Photographic Memories

Francis Frith's

Devon Churches

Martin Dunning

First published in the United Kingdom in 2001 by
Frith Book Company Ltd

Paperback Edition 2001
ISBN 1-85937-250-3

British Library Cataloguing in Publication Data

Francis Frith's Devon Churches
Martin Dunning

Frith Book Company Ltd
Frith's Barn, Teffont,
Salisbury, Wiltshire SP3 5QP
Tel: +44 (0) 1722 716 376
Email: info@francisfrith.co.uk
www.francisfrith.co.uk

Printed and bound in Great Britain

Front Cover: Torrington, The Church 24849

AS WITH ANY HISTORICAL DATABASE THE FRITH ARCHIVE IS CONSTANTLY BEING CORRECTED AND IMPROVED
AND THE PUBLISHERS WOULD WELCOME INFORMATION ON OMISSIONS OR INACCURACIES

Contents

Francis Frith: *Victorian Pioneer*

Francis Frith, Victorian founder of the world-famous photographic archive, was a complex and multi-talented man. A devout Quaker and a highly successful Victorian businessman, he was both philosophic by nature and pioneering in outlook.

By 1855 Francis Frith had already established a wholesale grocery business in Liverpool, and sold it for the astonishing sum of £200,000, which is the equivalent today of over £15,000,000. Now a multi-millionaire, he was able to indulge his passion for travel. As a child he had pored over travel books written by early explorers, and his fancy and imagination had been stirred by family holidays to the sublime mountain regions of Wales and Scotland. 'What a land of spirit-stirring and enriching scenes and places!' he had written. He was to return to these scenes of grandeur in later years to 'recapture the thousands of vivid and tender memories', but with a different purpose. Now in his thirties, and captivated by the new science of photography, Frith set out on a series of pioneering journeys to the Nile regions that occupied him from 1856 until 1860.

Intrigue and Adventure

He took with him on his travels a specially-designed wicker carriage that acted as both dark-room and sleeping chamber. These far-flung journeys were packed with intrigue and adventure. In his life story, written when he was sixty-three, Frith tells of being held captive by bandits, and of fighting 'an awful midnight battle to the very point of surrender with a deadly pack of hungry, wild dogs'. Sporting flowing Arab costume, Frith arrived at Akaba by camel seventy years before Lawrence, where he encountered 'desert princes and rival sheikhs, blazing with jewel-hilted swords'.

During these extraordinary adventures he was assiduously exploring the desert regions bordering the Nile and patiently recording the antiquities and peoples with his camera. He was the first photographer to venture beyond the sixth cataract. Africa was still the mysterious 'Dark Continent', and Stanley and Livingstone's historic meeting was a decade into the future. The conditions for picture taking confound belief. He laboured for hours in his wicker dark-room in the sweltering heat of the desert, while the volatile chemicals fizzed dangerously in their trays. Often he was forced to work in remote tombs and caves where conditions were cooler. Back in London he exhibited his photographs and was 'rapturously cheered' by members of the Royal Society. His reputation as a photographer was made overnight. An eminent modern historian has likened their impact on the population of the time to that on our own generation of the first photographs taken on the surface of the moon.

Venture of a Life-Time

Characteristically, Frith quickly spotted the opportunity to create a new business as a specialist publisher of photographs. He lived in an era of immense and sometimes violent change. For the poor in the early part of Victoria's reign work was a drudge and the hours long, and people had precious little free time to enjoy themselves. Most had no transport other than a cart or gig at their disposal, and had not travelled far beyond the boundaries of their own town or village. However, by the 1870s, the railways had threaded their way across the country, and Bank Holidays and half-day Saturdays had been made obligatory by Act of Parliament. All of a sudden the ordinary working man and his family were able to enjoy days out and see a little more of the world.

With characteristic business acumen, Francis Frith foresaw that these new tourists would enjoy having souvenirs to commemorate their days out. In 1860 he married Mary Ann Rosling and set out with the intention of photographing every city, town and village in Britain. For the next thirty years he travelled the country by train and by pony and trap, producing fine photographs of seaside resorts and beauty spots that were keenly bought by millions of Victorians. These prints were painstakingly pasted into family albums and pored over during the dark nights of winter, rekindling precious memories of summer excursions.

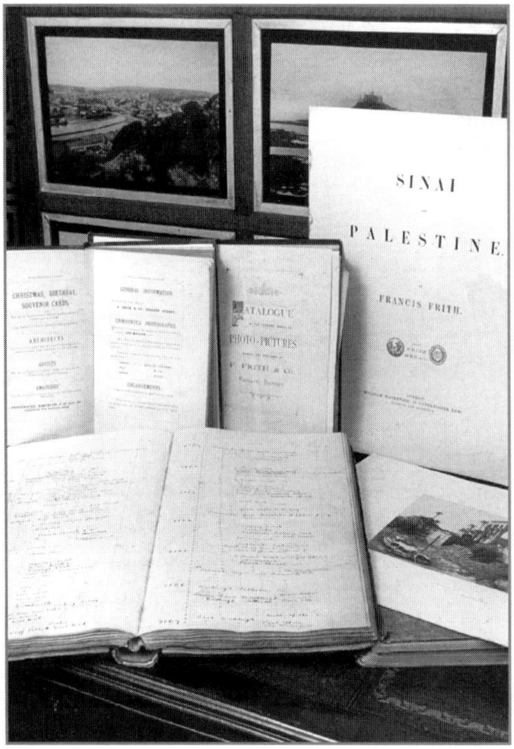

The Rise of Frith & Co

Frith's studio was soon supplying retail shops all over the country. To meet the demand he gathered about him a small team of photographers, and published the work of independent artist-photographers of the calibre of Roger Fenton and Francis Bedford. In order to gain some understanding of the scale of Frith's business one only has to look at the catalogue issued by Frith & Co in 1886: it runs to some 670 pages, listing not only many thousands of views of the British Isles but also many photographs of most European countries, and China, Japan, the USA and Canada – note the sample page shown opposite from the hand-written *Frith & Co* ledgers detailing pictures taken. By 1890 Frith had created the greatest specialist photographic publishing company in the

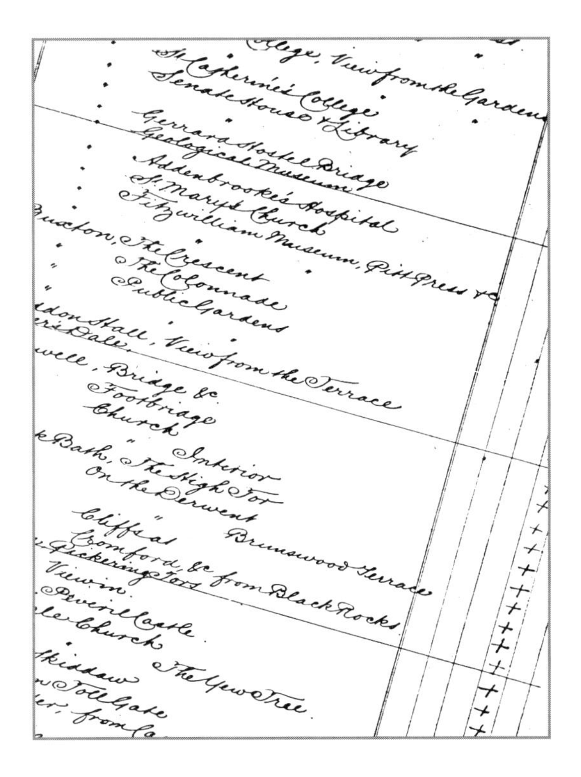

...llege, View from the Garden
St Catherine's College
Senate House & Library
Gerrards Hostel Bridge
Geological Museum
Addenbrooke's Hospital
St Mary's Church
Fitzwilliam Museum, Pitt Press &c
Buxton, The Crescent
The Colonnade
Public Gardens
...ddon Hall, View from the Terrace
...ri Dale
...well, Bridge &c
Footbridge
Church
" Interior
...Bath, The High Tor
On the Derwent
Cliffs at " Brunswood Terrace
Bomford, &c from Black Rocks
...Pickering Tor
View in
Peveril Castle
...le Church
...kiddaw The Yew Tree
...Toll Gate
...er, from Co...

world, with over 2,000 outlets – more than the combined number that Boots and WH Smith have today! The picture on the right shows the *Frith & Co* display board at Ingleton in the Yorkshire Dales. Beautifully constructed with mahogany frame and gilt inserts, it could display up to a dozen local scenes.

Postcard Bonanza

The ever-popular holiday postcard we know today took many years to develop. In 1870 the Post Office issued the first plain cards, with a pre-printed stamp on one face. In 1894 they allowed other publishers' cards to be sent through the mail with an attached adhesive halfpenny stamp. Demand grew rapidly, and in 1895 a new size of postcard was permitted called the court card, but there was little room for illustration. In 1899, a year after Frith's death, a new card measuring 5.5 x 3.5 inches became the standard format, but it was not until 1902 that the divided back came into being, with address and message on one face and a full-size illustration on the other. *Frith & Co* were in the vanguard of postcard development, and Frith's sons Eustace and Cyril continued their father's monumental task, expanding the number of views offered to the public and recording more and more places in Britain, as the coasts and countryside were opened up to mass travel.

Francis Frith died in 1898 at his villa in Cannes, his great project still growing. The archive he created continued in business for another seventy years. By 1970 it contained over a third of a million pictures of 7,000 cities, towns and villages. The massive photographic record Frith has left to us stands as a living monument to a special and very remarkable man.

Frith's Archive: *A Unique Legacy*

Francis Frith's legacy to us today is of immense significance and value, for the magnificent archive of evocative photographs he created provides a unique record of change in 7,000 cities, towns and villages throughout Britain over a century and more. Frith and his fellow studio photographers revisited locations many times down the years to update their views, compiling for us an enthralling and colourful pageant of British life and character.

We tend to think of Frith's sepia views of Britain as nostalgic, for most of us use them to conjure up memories of places in our own lives with which we have family associations. It often makes us forget that to Francis Frith they were records of daily life as it was actually being lived in the cities, towns and villages of his day. The Victorian age was one of great and often bewildering change for ordinary people, and though the pictures evoke an impression of slower times, life was as busy and hectic as it is today.

We are fortunate that Frith was a photographer of the people, dedicated to recording the minutiae of everyday life. For it is this sheer wealth of visual data, the painstaking chronicle of changes in dress, transport, street layouts, buildings, housing, engineering and landscape that captivates us so much today. His remarkable images offer us a powerful link with the past and with the lives of our ancestors.

See Frith at www. francisfrith.co.uk

Today's Technology

Computers have now made it possible for Frith's many thousands of images to be accessed almost instantly. In the Frith archive today, each photograph is carefully 'digitised' then stored on a CD Rom. Frith archivists can locate a single photograph amongst thousands within seconds. Views can be catalogued and sorted under a variety of categories of place and content to the immediate benefit of researchers.

Inexpensive reference prints can be created for them at the touch of a mouse button, and a wide range of books and other printed materials assembled and published for a wider, more general readership - in the next twelve months over a hundred Frith local history titles will be published! The day-to-day workings of the archive are very different from how they were in Francis Frith's time: imagine the herculean task of sorting through eleven tons of glass negatives as Frith had to do to locate a particular sequence of pictures! Yet the archive still prides itself on maintaining the same high standards of excellence laid down by Francis Frith, including the painstaking cataloguing and indexing of every view.

It is curious to reflect on how the internet now allows researchers in America and elsewhere greater instant access to the archive than Frith himself ever enjoyed. Many thousands of individual views can be called up on screen within seconds on one of the Frith internet sites, enabling people living continents away to revisit the streets of their ancestral home town, or view places in Britain where they have enjoyed holidays. Many overseas researchers welcome the chance to view special theme selections, such as transport, sports, costume and ancient monuments.

We are certain that Francis Frith would have heartily approved of these modern developments in imaging techniques, for he himself was always working at the very limits of Victorian photographic technology.

The Value of the Archive Today

Because of the benefits brought by the computer, Frith's images are increasingly studied by social historians, by researchers into genealogy and ancestory, by architects, town planners, and by teachers and schoolchildren involved in local history projects.

In addition, the archive offers every one of us an opportunity to examine the places where we and our families have lived and worked down the years. Highly successful in Frith's own era, the archive is now, a century and more on, entering a new phase of popularity.

The Past in Tune with the Future

Historians consider the Francis Frith Collection to be of prime national importance. It is the only archive of its kind remaining in private ownership and has been valued at a million pounds. However, this figure is now rapidly increasing as digital technology enables more and more people around the world to enjoy its benefits.

Francis Frith's archive is now housed in an historic timber barn in the beautiful village of Teffont in Wiltshire. Its founder would not recognize the archive office as it is today. In place of the many thousands of dusty boxes containing glass plate negatives and an all-pervading odour of photographic chemicals, there are now ranks of computer screens. He would be amazed to watch his images travelling round the world at unimaginable speeds through network and internet lines.

The archive's future is both bright and exciting. Francis Frith, with his unshakeable belief in making photographs available to the greatest number of people, would undoubtedly approve of what is being done today with his lifetime's work. His photographs, depicting our shared past, are now bringing pleasure and enlightenment to millions around the world a century and more after his death.

Devon Churches - *An Introduction*

DURING AN EXCAVATION near South Street in Exeter in 1945, a small black piece of 4th-century pottery was found bearing the chi-rho symbol, this being a representation of the first two letters of the Greek name for Christ. It is the earliest Christian artefact to have been found in Devon; its origin is unknown, but its presence indicates that at this early time, pockets of the new religion had become established even in the farthest-flung reaches of the Roman Empire.

A more widespread incursion of Christianity into the south-west came with the Celtic missionaries of the 5th and 6th centuries. The first recorded is St Samson, who came to Cornwall circa 520. He was followed by men who, in spreading the Gospel, left their mark in place names and the dedication of churches. Thus Braunton takes its name from the Welshman St Brannoc, Landkey commemorates St Kea, and Filliegh, just down the road, is named after his travelling companion St Filli. The most widely travelled of these Celtic missionaries seems to have been the ubiquitous Petroc, to whom eighteen churches are dedicated across the county from Dartmouth in the south to Parracombe in the north.

By the 7th century, the Saxons were pushing

westwards, bringing with them the Roman church. In AD690 they established an abbey at Exeter, which was attended by, among others, St Boniface, who was born plain Wynfrith at Crediton but went on to become patron saint of Germany. However, resistance to the new church was high and as late as AD700 St Aldhelm complained that Devon priests were still using old Celtic customs rather than Roman ones.

At this time, Devon did not have its own bishop - being part of the Diocese of Sherborne in Dorset - but in AD890 King Athelstan appointed Asser as Bishop, and in AD1049 Leofric was given the joint See of Crediton and Cornwall. With Crediton being out in the wilds, Leofric moved his seat to the growing port city of Exeter, creating the Diocese of Exeter which was to remain the sole seat of ecclesiastical power in Devon and Cornwall for the next 800 years.

Physical remains of the Saxon church in Devon are few and far between. St Giles at Sidbury has a Saxon crypt, and excavations at Bere Ferrers have uncovered the remains of what was probably a Saxon church. However, Saxon churches were built of cob, or from wood with a thatched roof, and were unlikely to have lasted over the centuries. As it is, most were swept away in the first great period of English church-building, which was carried out by the Normans.

The Norman nobles who received vast estates from a grateful William the Conqueror built churches in the style of their homeland. Although more accomplished than their Saxon counterparts, Norman masons were unsure of the properties of the stone with which they worked. To be on the safe side (for reasons of defence as well as structural integrity) they built their walls thick and kept the windows small; larger windows would have weakened the structure. Their arches, following the Roman model, were semi-circular, and the overall effect was of squat, powerful buildings.

Rebuilding over the centuries has disguised and erased many Norman churches, but Norman components can still be seen here and there. Fonts seem to have survived well, such as those at St Marychurch in Torquay and St Margaret's at Topsham, and Norman doorways, with their characteristic round arches, can be seen at St James' in Parkham and St John's in Paignton. The latter (photograph 25472, page 61) also shows the abstract geometrical carving of which Norman masons were so fond.

Perhaps the grandest examples of Norman architecture in Devon are the twin towers (photograph 19603, page 89) of Exeter Cathedral, built by Bishop Warlewast in the first half of the 12th century. These majestic towers exhibit the Norman arch in their windows, but a look at the windows of the east front, and at the Purbeck stone columns of the nave (photograph 37998, page 89) reveals that their arches are pointed. Exeter Cathedral straddles the transitional period between

Norman and Gothic church-building.

The pointed arch is a fundamental of the Gothic style, and its arrival from the continent in the latter half of the 12th century was to radically change the atmosphere of churches. Because of its greater strength, the pointed arch could support huge loads and therefore allow larger windows and airier arcades. No longer were churches the gloomy, almost claustrophobic spaces they had been in Norman times; architects were able to give their imaginations free rein, whether creating the glory of the nave at Exeter or the simple beauty of the Beer Stone arcade at All Saints, Malborough.

All this building cost money, however. By 1100 the Bishop of Exeter was the biggest landowner in Devon after the King and the Sheriff, holding 24 manors covering 77,000 acres, and 11 manors in Cornwall. Rents and tithes from his holdings kept the Bishop's coffers in funds for his own projects, and if a particular town or village wanted a new aisle or better tower there was probably a rich patron available.

Patronage was a cornerstone of church affairs. For the humble parishioner it ensured (albeit at a cost) that they had a church in which to worship and therefore save their immortal souls, while for the patron the benefits were twofold. Rich landowners such as the Rolles on the south coast or the Fulfords of Dunsford were entitled, as patrons, to appoint the rector and take the profits generated by rents and tithes. This money, used to endow a new chapel or aisle and pay a priest to say masses for the soul, ensured a trouble-free time in the afterlife for the patron concerned. At its extreme, patronage led to the construction of chantries, dedicated solely to the spiritual benefit of men such as Guy de Bryan, whose chantry tower still stands at Slapton.

Individuals were not the only patrons; great priories such as that at Plympton, and abbeys like Tavistock, the richest in the county, were major landowners and patrons of many churches including St Helen's at Abbotsham, which had become part of the endowment of Tavistock Abbey in the 10th century. This constant endowment was a spur to building and the simple Norman churches were extended and rebuilt many times between the 14th and early 16th centuries.

The buildings also became more complex as ritual developed - by the late 13th century Christ was thought to be physically present in the bread and wine at Mass, and it was considered only right to screen off the chancel from the rude and sweaty populace. Thus came about the screen that is such a feature of Devon churches. These were carved from wood, as at St Michael's, Ilsington, and occasionally of stone, as at St Mary's of Totnes (photograph 38232, page 52).

At the turn of the 14th century there were over 400 churches in Devon, looking very different

inside from the churches we know today. Colour would have dominated - in wall-paintings, stained glass, rich vestments and hangings - and the church, as well as being a place of worship, would have been the scene of many a rowdy public assembly, along with theatre, music, processions and even market stalls.

In 1517 Martin Luther famously nailed his 95 theses to the door of the church in Wittenburg, igniting the glowing ember of resentment towards the power and corruption of the Roman church. Henry VIII may not have shared Luther's theological views - in fact he was fairly orthodox in spiritual matters - but he too was tired of the power of Rome. The English Reformation that followed his protracted battle with the Pope over the annulment of his marriage to Catherine of Aragon, culminating in the Act of Supremacy in 1534, was to bring about the biggest change since the arrival of the Normans.

The monasteries were an obvious target, for as well as being highly resistant to the new order of things, they were also immensely wealthy. Tavistock Abbey and Plympton Priory both had incomes of over £900 in 1534, but the dissolutions of 1536 and 1539 swept them away, and their wealth and power fell into the hands of the King's favourites. Over the next century, until the process was completed under Elizabeth, symbols of the old religion were suppressed: stained glass was smashed, walls whitewashed, altars destroyed and statues toppled.

In Devon, an outpost where resistance to change was strong, congregations and clergy balked at Edward VI's introduction in 1549 of the Mass in English and the Book of Common Prayer. The Prayer Book Rebellion started at Sampford Courtenay and moved on to Crediton where it met up with a band of Cornish rebels. The throng laid siege to Exeter but were defeated at the Battle of Fenny Bridges near Honiton. The leaders, men like mill owner John Bury from Harford on the River Yealm, were hunted down and executed. Despite the Reformation, some Devon families clung to the old religion: the Courtenays of Powderham, the Carys of Torre and the Cliffords of Ugbrooke were among those practising in secret.

The upheavals were not over, however. The Civil War divided the county, setting father against son, brother against brother and even clergy against flock; Rev John Snell of Thurlestone was chaplain to Charles I and upon returning to his parish after the war he was hounded out by Parliamentarian locals. At Torrington, the Church of St Michael (photograph 75108, page 99) was spectacularly obliterated; the Puritan aftermath destroyed almost as much church art as the Reformation had in the previous century. Some was saved by clever subterfuge: the Norman font at St Marychurch was upended to hide its elaborate carving and Bovey Tracey's eagle lectern spent years hidden in a pond to protect it from destruction.

In the 18th century, with the great building sprees of Norman and Gothic long over, and the crises of Reformation and Civil War survived (albeit at some cost), the church settled into a period of stagnation, even decline. The Bishops were no longer quite the power they had been, and patronage in the new church seemed to offer less hope of guaranteed admission to the sweet hereafter. Church building and restoration dwindled to almost nothing, although there are one or two Georgian gems such as the delightful, unspoilt interior of St Petrock's at Parracombe.

Congregations also dwindled, and this was partly due to the absence of clergy. A survey of 1768 records that, of the 604 parishes in Devon, almost half were served by absentee incumbents. This air of apathy did the fabric of churches no good, and by the 19th century many were in a hopeless condition. St Peter's at Barnstaple, for instance, was by 1860 'in a ruinous state, with bulging walls and sinking roofs.' Nonconformism also played a part, with Baptists and Quakers offering an alternative to the established church and siphoning off a few souls here and there. In 1743 John Wesley and his brother Charles brought Methodism to Devon, but met with little success and moved on to more fertile pastures in Cornwall.

The 19th century saw the appearance of the wealthy men who, although holding the title of parson, acted more like squires and had an eye for the more earthly pursuits. By the time Bishop Philpotts took over the Diocese in 1831 there were twenty of these 'Squarsons' who had their own packs of hounds and hunted several times a week. Some, like Jack Russell of Swimbridge, tempered their activities with a genuine concern for their flock; others were not so conscientious and Hoskins reports that the 'unspeakable oaf' Parson Froude of Knowstone 'left his parish in a heathen and lawless condition.'

There were, however, genuine reformers who were encouraged by Bishop Philpotts. These included men like Rev Edward Girdlestone, vicar of Halberton from 1863-72, who inveighed from the pulpit against the treatment of farm labourers, making himself extremely unpopular with landowners. However, he eventually improved wages and conditions for the workers.

The revival of the Church of England's fortunes in the 19th century was due in part to the zeal of men like Bishop Philpotts, who were spurred on by the Oxford Movement's demands for a return to traditional values and customs, and in part to the urban growth that caused a lack of pew space. By the 1840s there were over thirty churches under construction in Devon - more than at any other time before or since - and many more were undergoing renovation. The return to traditional values led to the Victorian Gothic Revival; architects were in demand and men like Edward Ashcroft,

Benjamin Ferrey and Sir George Gilbert Scott moved from commission to commission. Sometimes, as with Ferrey's Church of St Mary in Barnstaple (photograph 69316, page 102), they started from scratch, while elsewhere they renovated older structures.

Not all renovations were sensitively executed. Many original features were unceremoniously ripped out, such as the loft at St Mary's Totnes, and the heavy-handedness of the restorers and designers produced results that have variously been described as 'melancholy' and 'cruel'. The former is the modern opinion of the renowned Devon historian W G Hoskins on St Mary's, Rockbeare; the latter is a contemporary assessment by Rev Sabine Baring-Gould of the restoration of St Edward's at Shaugh Prior, ironically carried out by one Ewan Christian.

Despite the machine-made, mass-produced wood and stone windows and pews used by the Victorians, which lack the craftsmanship or outright artistry of earlier times, some Victorian churches are impressive edifices. St Marychurch (photograph 69605, pages 62-63), which dominates the skyline of Torquay, is a fitting monument to what is reputed to be the oldest church site in Devon. St Peter's in Shaldon (photograph 54072, page 72), built in red sandstone with darker polyphant stone dressings, is actually quite beautiful. Even the nonconformists were carried along by the flamboyant zeal of Victorian architects, erecting striking churches like Mutley Baptist (photograph 22421, page 24).

The 20th century saw little more church-building, but a further crisis arose from the attentions of the Luftwaffe. St Andrew's in Plymouth was severely damaged but was rebuilt and reconsecrated in 1957, its modern altar and panes of stained glass blending with the older fabric of the original buildings. St Andrew's layers of history in stone, wood and glass, built on a site used for worship as far back as the 8th century, are typical of the story of churches in Devon - swept by the tides of history, but surviving invasion, war and the whims of Kings.

West Devon and Dartmoor

Bere Ferrers and River Tavy 1898 42258
St Andrew's was built by the powerful de Ferrers family in the 13th and 14th centuries. The first rector was Reginald de Ferrers in 1258. This may have been the site of a far earlier church, for in 1980 excavations uncovered a building near the south-east corner which is thought to have been a Saxon church.

Lamerton, St Peter's Church interior 1890 22566
The 14th-15th century Church of St Peter was restored in 1876 at a cost of £1,396 3s 6d. On 11 November 1877 there was a fire: 'The roof fell in with a terrible crash, and shortly afterwards the four arches on the eastern side, and the massive granite pillars from which they sprang, were so scorched with the heat that the whole fell against the northern wall ...' The church was restored again and opened on 29 January 1880.

Tavistock, Brent Tor 1890 22557
'A church, full bleak, and weather beaten, all alone as if it were forsaken.' So wrote Devon chronicler Tristram Ridson in 1625, and the Church of St Michael de Rupe, sitting atop its volcanic plug high above the surrounding landscape, certainly has an isolated feel to it. It is now used only occasionally, a new church having been built in the village below in 1856.

Horrabridge St John's Church and Village 1898 42242
St John the Baptist was originally a daughter church of Buckland Abbey and is mentioned as far back as 1438 in Bishop Lacy's register. The present church was built on the site of the old chapel in 1892-93, its construction made possible by a donation of £1,000 by Sir Massey Lopes of Maristow.

Tavistock Church Interior 1890 22544

Tavistock grew up around the great Benedictine Abbey, the richest in Devon, that was founded in the 10th century. It went the way of all abbeys at the dissolution of the monasteries, but its remains can still be seen near the parish church - St Eustachius, which was dedicated in 1318 and rebuilt in the 14th century.

Princetown St Michael and All Angels Church 1931 84062

St Michael and All Angels stands on this bleak spot 1,400 feet above sea level. Work commenced on the church in 1810, carried out by French prisoners of war for 6d a day, and was completed by American prisoners in 1813-16. The church fell into disrepair and was badly damaged by fire in 1868, but was restored in 1898 and 1908. In 1912 Princetown became a parish in its own right.

Stoke, The Church of St Andrew and St Mary 1890 22459

There has probably been a church here for a thousand years, high on the hill overlooking the creek that once flowed from Stonehouse to Pennycomequick. The Church of St Andrew and St Mary has parts of the tower and porches that are 15th century; the rest dates from 1751, when it was enlarged to cater for the growing population working in the dockyard.

Stoke, Church Interior 1890 22472
The organ was moved to this position in 1873 when the gallery was removed. In 1883 chairs replaced the box pews and a year later the organ was rebuilt, lasting until 1977 when the theft of lead from the roof caused it to suffer water damage and necessitated a further rebuild.

Plymouth, St Andrew's Church 1889 22399
Construction of St Andrew's started in 1370 and the tower was built by Thomas Yogge in 1481. Its status as the mother church of Plymouth could not protect it from the Luftwaffe and in 1941 it was reduced to a shell. Restoration started in 1949 and St Andrew's was eventually reconsecrated in 1957.

Plymouth St Andrew's Cross 1900 45862
While St Andrew's was still a smoking ruin, someone wrote the word Resurgam (Latin for 'I will rise again') above the door of the north porch (left), and ever since it has been known as the Resurgam Door. St Andrew's Cross (behind the policeman) was also destroyed in the Blitz, and all that remains is the copper cross from the top, now displayed in the north aisle.

Plymouth Mutley Baptist Chapel Interior 1890 22422

The first pastor here was Rev Benwell Bird, who held the post for 23 years and was very popular, not only with his own flock, but with all denominations. Mutley Baptist was, miraculously, undamaged during the Second World War, whereas George Street Baptist was destroyed in 1941 and eventually rebuilt on Catherine Street.

Plymouth, Mutley Baptist Chapel 1890 22421
The Palladian splendour of Mutley Baptist Chapel dates from 1869. George Street Baptist, near St Andrew's, was bursting at the seams and so a new daughter church was built at Mutley. By 1876 it had broken away from George Street and become a congregation in its own right.

Plymouth, St Peter's Church 1889 45868

In 1830 Rev John Hawker resigned as curate at Stoke Damerell and founded a chapel here which eventually became the parish church of the new parish of St Peter's. The chancel was built in 1850 and the nave and chapel in 1882. In 1903 a copper spire was added in memory of George Rundle Prynne, vicar from 1848-1903. The Blitz gutted the church and during restoration the gables were removed.

Plymouth, St Peter's Church Chancel 1889 22404
The restoration of St Peter's (by Frederick Etchells, who also did St Andrew's) changed the appearance of the interior considerably. The modern St Peter's is far simpler than in this picture - the screen is gone, and the ornamental lights have been replaced with plainer fittings.

Plymouth, Charles Church 1889 22405
The building of Charles Church started in 1640 after Charles I gave permission for another parish to be created. Construction was suspended in the Civil War and completed in 1657. It was dedicated to King Charles the Martyr in 1665. Once one of the finest post-Reformation Gothic churches in the country, Charles Church was gutted in the blitz and the ruins retained as a memorial to Plymouth's war dead.

Plymouth, Catholic Cathedral Altar 1889 22411
There was a Catholic chapel here as early as 1806, but the cathedral of St Mary and St Boniface was built by Bishop Vaughan in 1858 and consecrated in 1860. The architects were Joseph and Charles Hansom (Joseph designed the Hansom Cab) and in 1867 the 207-foot spire was added.

Plymouth, Roman Catholic Cathedral, Lady Chapel 1889 22412
The Lady Chapel was restored in 1921 and, in addition to Mary, contains four other stone figures: King David, the Saints Joachim and Anne, and John the Baptist.

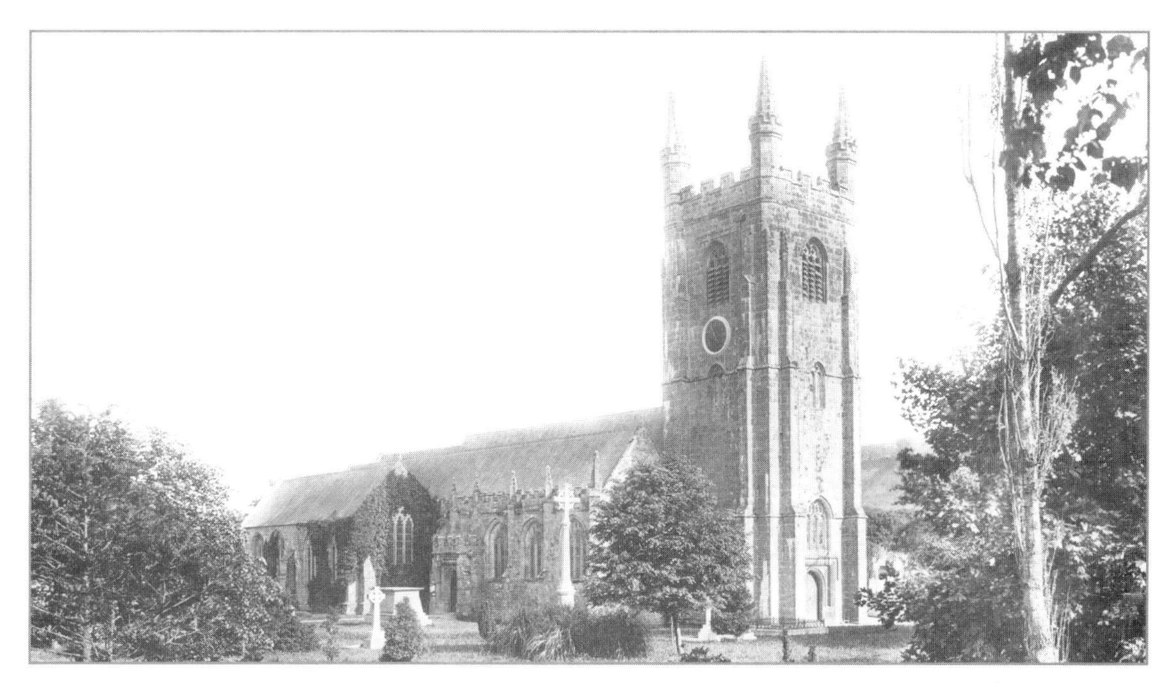

Plympton, St Mary's Church 1898 41946
There has been a church here since the reign of King Alfred, dedicated at first to Saints Peter and Paul. The present church, dedicated to St Mary, was originally a chapel to the rich Augustinian Priory that was established here in 1127. The chancel dates from the 14th century and the handsome 108-foot tower from the 15th century.

Plympton, St Mary's Church Reredos 1898 22501
This reredos is a modern addition depicting the Adoration of the Shepherds (left) and the Entombment of Christ. On the north side of the north chapel is a tomb in memory of Richard Strode (died 1464); this bears an unusual representation of the Holy Trinity, showing God holding a crucifix between his knees and a dove at the top of the cross. This 'Italian Trinity' was very popular between the 12th and 17th centuries. The only other one in Devon is at Ashwater.

Shaugh Prior, The Village c1965 S356018
Construction of the Church of St Edward, King and Martyr was commenced in the 14th century but the building was not completed until the late 15th or early 16th centuries. It was restored in 1868 by Ewan Christian, an act which Rev Sabine Baring Gould described as 'cruel'. Among other things, Christian threw out the beautiful 15th-century font cover; this was rescued in 1870 from a nearby linhay, but not before the farmer's wife had tried to get her husband to burn it.

Ivybridge, Old Church 1890 22522
With the building of St John's in 1882 the old chapel fell into disuse, as can be seen in the cloak of ivy. It was eventually bought in 1925 for £5 by a Mr H Blight and demolished for its stone, which was re-used for houses.

Ashburton Grammar School 1907 58537
The chapel of St Lawrence was once the private chapel of the Bishops of Exeter, who had a house in Ashburton. In 1314 Bishop Stapleton granted the chapel to the town, and a priest started a school here which ran until 1937. In 1983 Dartmoor National Park took over the building, restoring it in 1986-88.

Ashburton Church Interior 1907
58536
The first church here was built by Ethelward de Pomeroy in 1137, and part of the porch still dates from that time. The rest of the church was rebuilt in the 13th-15th centuries. A local custom was that at weddings the bride entered by the north porch and left by the south. This no longer happens, as the south porch is now a window.

Buckfastleigh
Buckfast Abbey c1955
B238030
The Abbey was built between 1882 and 1932 on the site of the 10th-century abbey that was dissolved in 1537. Benedictine monks did every bit of work themselves - even constructing the 158-foot tower - using local limestone.

Dartmoor, Widecombe in the Moor, The Church of St Pancras 1907 5805
The Cathedral of the Moors, as the 14th century Church of St Pancras is known, stands in an enormous parish of 11,000 acres. In 1638 a thunderbolt hit the church, killing four worshippers and injuring sixty-two.

Ilsington, The Village and Church c1965 18009
The Church of St Michael was built in the 14th century and enlarged in the 15th century. It has a 16th-century rood screen and a clergy stall of carved medieval bench-ends. The latter are decorated with the only carved poppy-heads in Devon. In 1586 the Elizabethan dramatist John Ford was baptised here.

Bovey Tracey, The Parish Church c1955 b161008
The dedication to Saints Peter and Paul and St Thomas of Canterbury is explained by the fact that William de Tracey, who held the manor, was one of the knights involved in the killing of Thomas à Becket at Canterbury in 1170. The tower is 14th-century and the nave and chancel 15th-century. The north aisle was added in 1858.

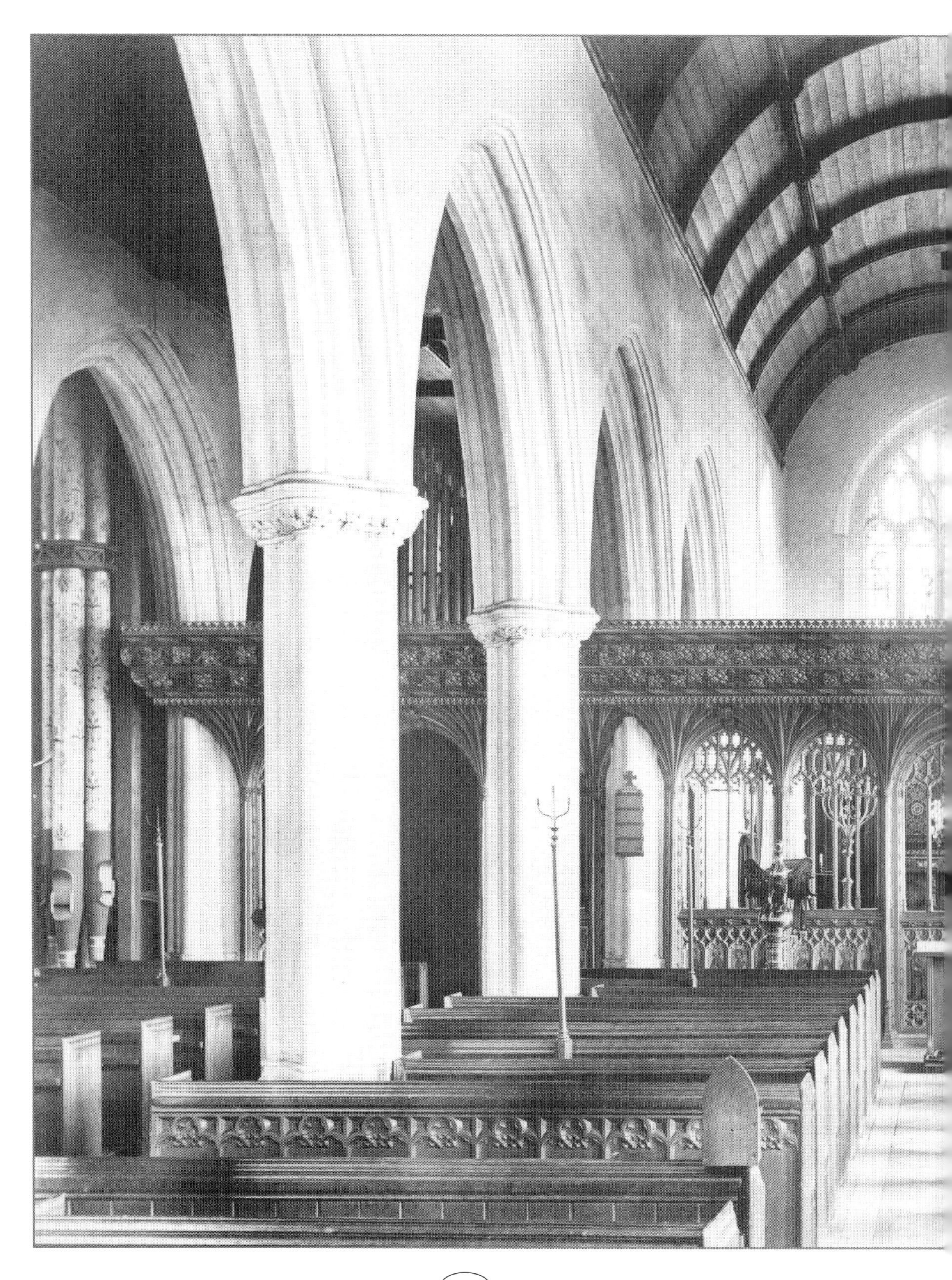

Bovey Tracey
The Church Interior
1907 58527
The 15th-century screen is one of the finest in Devon. The stone pulpit, also 15th-century, has figures of St Peter, Edward the Confessor, St George and St Margaret of Antioch. The 15th-century eagle lectern was removed during the Civil War by Rev James Forbes and hidden in a pond.

Lustleigh St John's Church c1955 L115046

St John the Baptist was built between the 13th and 16th centuries. However, it has a red granite stone dating from the 8th or 9th century and on this is an inscription, perhaps in Welsh, which has so far proved indecipherable.

◄ **North Bovey Church interior 1907**

58513

The wagon roof has wooden bosses that are possibly 13th-century. The designs of these bosses include the Tinners' Rabbits - three rabbits sharing only three ears. This was the alchemical symbol for tin and is also said to represent the Holy Trinity.

North Bovey
St John's Church 1907
58511
St John the Baptist was obviously a popular saint in these parts, for this is another church dedicated to him. It dates from the 15th century although the chancel and lower tower may be 13th-century.

Dunsford
St Mary's Church c1960
D118010
The first vicar of St Mary's was Thomas de Bonville in the early 14th century. The church was built in the 14th and 15th centuries and the chancel rebuilt in 1844-5. The pulpit, altar rails and west gallery all date from the late 17th and early 18th centuries.

Dunsford
Church Interior
Fulford Tomb c1960
D118014
This elaborately carved tomb with its Corinthian pillars is the resting place of Sir Thomas Fulford (died 1610) and his wife Ursula, who outlived him by 25 years. Fulford, a couple of miles from Dunsford, was a Domesday manor and the Fulford family have been there since the reign of Richard I.

◄ **Drewsteignton**
The Village c1880
5800
The Church of the Holy Trinity was built from granite in the 15th and 16th centuries and has a Jacobean pulpit and the arms of Queen Elizabeth over the south door. The chancel was rebuilt in 1863 and at the same time the screen was removed.

Dunsford
The Church Interior c1960 D118012
The oak pews are a relatively new addition, built in 1933. In the corner, above the tomb, hang the sword and helmet of one of the Fulfords - a fitting reminder of this family of soldiers who sent three of their sons to the Crusades.

Chagford
St Michael's Church 1931 83909
The Church of St Michael the Archangel was first dedicated by Bishop Branscombe in 1261 and rebuilt in the 15th century. The churchyard contains the grave of James Perrot, who placed the first letterbox on Dartmoor at Cranmere Pool, unwittingly starting a craze which has reached ridiculous proportions, with over 8,000 letterboxes today.

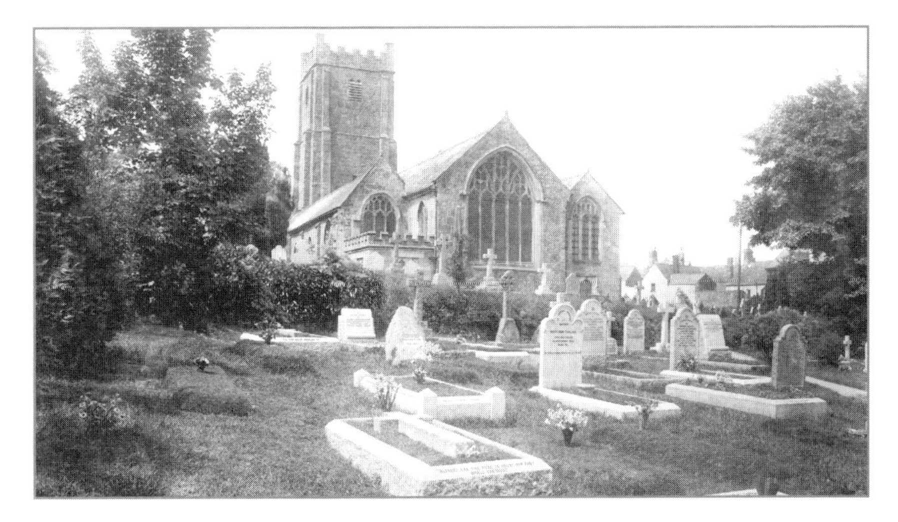

Chagford
St Michael's Church Interior 1931 83910
The roof bosses here include the three-eared rabbit, as seen at North Bovey and Widecombe. To the left of the altar, and just visible in this photograph, is the exotically carved, white stone tomb of Sir John Whiddon (died 1575).

South Devon

Newton Ferrers, from Noss Mayo 1890 22487
St Peter's was built in the 1880s by Lord Revelstoke, a member of the Baring banking family. The church stands almost exactly opposite the Church of the Holy Cross in Newton Ferrers.

Yealmpton
The Church 1904 52430

The parish is first mentioned in 1225 when the Bishop of Exeter agreed with the Bishop of Salisbury to swap the parishes of Kenton and West Alvington for those of Kingsteignton and Yealmpton. In 1334 the induction of an absentee vicar, Sir John de Flesio of Genoa, led to protests by parishioners who only backed down when threatened with excommunication.

Modbury
Memorial, Catholic and Parish Churches c1960 M172022

The 18th-century congregation at St George's seem to have been model citizens: 'The greatest orniment is the behaviour of the congregation in time of worship, which an ancient clergyman, who happened to officiate at the communion some years since, declared to be the most decent and becoming he had ever seen.' The Roman Catholic Church of St Monica's (right) was built in 1967.

◀ **Ringmore Church interior 1907**
58122
All Hallows looks down on the beautiful Ayrmer Cove. Note the curious little circular window on the left. It is said that in the days of smugglers, a light was shone from this window to guide the smugglers' vessels safely into the cove.

Ringmore All Hallows Church c1960 R258015

The list of rectors of the 13th-century church of All Hallows goes back to 1257 and includes the name of one William Lane, who was actually rector of Aveton Gifford. Lane, a vociferous Royalist, spent three months hiding from the Roundheads in the tower of All Hallows.

Thurlestone All Saints Church 1904 52454

The first church on this site was built in the 12th century from cob and timber with a thatched roof. The present church of All Saints dates from the early 13th century and was enlarged in the 15th century. Subsidence led to the tower tilting eastwards, and the Victorian vicar Rev Peregrine Ilbert rebuilt the upper part, producing the kink in the tower that is visible from some angles.

Aveton Gifford St Andrew's Church 1890 24534

The 13th-century church of St Andrew's was rebuilt in 1957, having been destroyed by bombing on 25 January 1943. The bombing was probably accidental, for Aveton Gifford is hardly big enough to represent a strategic target.

Malborough, All Saints Church 1927 79907
The church here was founded circa 1200 and the building dates from the 13th century. Its name, All Saints, has only been in use since the 19th century and there is some doubt as to what the original dedication was. The spire and tower were rendered with cement in 1853 to counteract the porosity of the stone from which they are built.

Malborough, All Saints Church 1927 79908
The columns are of Beer stone, an expensive commodity that is rarely found this far west in Devon. It was probably landed at Kingsbridge or Salcombe and was then carted from sea level to 400 feet above - something of an undertaking and a test of the builders' faith.

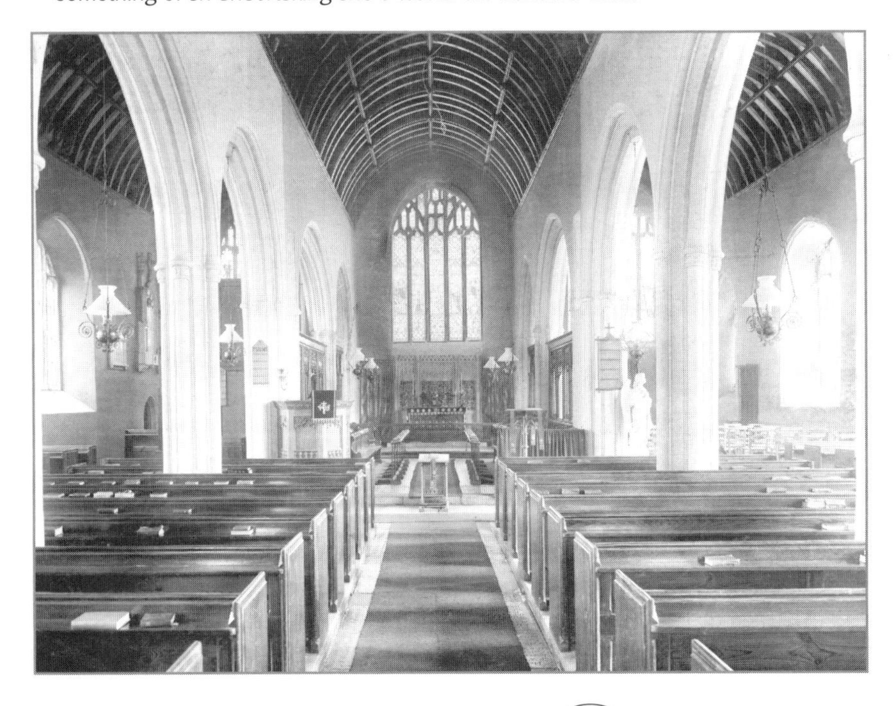

Kingsbridge Dodbrooke Church 1904 52450
The tower of Thomas à Becket dates from the 14th century and the rest of the church from the 15th century. It originally had a spire but this was removed in 1785. The list of rectors goes back to 1327 and their names are recorded on shields on the 15th-16th-century screen.

Sherford St Martin's Chrurch 1890 25272

St Martin's is a daughter church of Stokenham. It probably evolved from the licensed chapels at nearby Keynedon and Malston farms that are recorded in 1370. The church was consecrated in 1457 and has a carved chancel screen that has never been restored; it is still possible to see the original brush strokes.

▼ **East Portlemouth, Church 1925** 78402
The Church of St Winwalloe, or Onolaus, was built in the 15th century onto an earlier tower. The screen has the usual evangelists and saints, and also the figure of Sir John Schorn, a Buckinghamshire rector who was reputed to have caught the devil and imprisoned him in a boot. Until the Reformation he was regarded as a patron against ague and gout.

▼ **Dartington, St Mary's Church c1890** D4032
Built in local stone from Shinner's Bridge quarry and designed by John Loughborough Pearson, architect of Truro Cathedral, St Mary the Virgin was consecrated in 1880 by Bishop Temple, who later became Archbishop of Canterbury. The church replaced the 15th-century one in the grounds of Dartington Hall, of which only the tower now remains.

▲ **Dartington St Mary's Church Interior c1890** D4301
St Mary was built to the ground plan of the old church, and incorporates some of its fabric: the font of Dartmoor granite, which is the oldest part of the church; the High Altar; and the Beer stone arcades, which are mounted on Portland stone bases to increase the height of the nave.

◄ **Totnes Parish Church 1896**

38229

There was almost certainly a church here in the time of King Edgar's mint (AD958-75) but the present building dates from the 15th century. Construction was hampered by a series of disputes between the monks and townsfolk, and the process was only speeded up in 1434 when Bishop Lacy offered an indulgence to all who contributed.

Totnes, The Parish Church Chancel 1896 38232
The magnificent carved stone chancel screen dates from 1459 and is almost unique. The tower was also built in 1459, and a special quay was built at the bottom of the street to land the stone.

Dittisham, St George's Church c1960 D34015
How many people lie buried in the average churchyard? Well, in the case of St George's it has been calculated that 18,000 bodies have been interred here since 1180. The nave and chancel were rebuilt in 1328-33 and the tower is older.

Dartmouth, The Church Door 1889 21606

St Saviour's was founded by Edward I in 1286 and enlarged and rebuilt in the 15th and 17th centuries. The 15th-century rebuilding was undertaken by John Hawley, merchant, adventurer and the model for the English sailor in Chaucer's Canterbury tales. This door in the south porch is decorated with 13th-century ironwork.

Dartmouth
The Castle and Mouth of Dart, with St Petrock's Church c1885 2536g
Dartmouth Castle, built in 1481 to deter Breton raiders, shares its headland with St Petrock's Church, which was built in the 17th century. It has a plastered wagon roof and three early 17th-century brasses at the east end of the south aisle.

Kingswear, The Church 1890 25292
The Church of Thomas a Becket is thought to have received its dedication because of its proximity to a landing place for pilgrims bound for Canterbury. The original 15th-century church was rebuilt in 1847 at a cost of £1,280.

Stokenham, The Church c1960 S197046
St Michael and All Angels is a common dedication for churches, like Stokenham's, built on high ground. The 14th-century church was first dedicated to St Humbert the Confessor and then St Barnabas before receiving its current dedication in 1421.

Slapton, St James's Church and Chantry Tower 1890 25265
In the background is the ruined tower of the chantry church founded in 1327 by Sir Guy de Bryan, one of the first Knights of the Garter. St James (right) was dedicated by Bishop Stapledon in 1318, and an altar slab stone found recently is thought to be the very stone involved in that dedication.

Brixham, All Saints Church 1906 54039a
The first church here was built in 1824, but in 1872 the roof blew off in a storm and Rev R B F Elrington commenced a rebuilding that was to take until 1907. The handsome seven-light window in the west front (right) was built in 1892 in memory of a Mrs Hogg.

Stoke Gabriel, The Creek c1965 S366049
The Church of St Mary and St Gabriel was mentioned as early as 1148 by Bishop Robert Chichester, and the present building is thought to have been built slightly after the 14th-century tower. A restoration in 1855 under Rev Robert Bowden removed most of the carved medieval bench ends.

Stoke Gabriel, The Yew Tree c1965 S366023
This enormous and venerable yew tree is mentioned in the Domesday Book as being hundreds of years old, so its age now is anybody's guess, but it has probably been here for 1,500 years.

Paignton, St John's Church 1889 21533
Built from the local Old Red sandstone, St John's stands near the remains of the palace of the Bishops of Exeter, who kept a deer park here. The arcades are late 13th-century and the porch is 14th-century.

Paignton, The Church Screen 1889 21536
This late 15th-century chantry screen is a monument to the Kirkham family, whose tombs lie underneath the two ornate arches. Although damaged by the less than caring attentions of human hands in past centuries, it remains one of the finest examples of its type in the country.

Paignton, St John's Church, Norman Door 1890 25472
St John's has Norman masonry in the chancel and a Norman font, but the most striking Norman component is this fine door set in the west wall of the 15th-century tower, making good use of the contrast between pale Beer stone and Old Red sandstone.

▼ Torquay, Tormohun Church 1889 21473

The Church of St Saviour at Tormohun has a 14th-century tower, and the rest is 15th-century. The chancel was enlarged in 1873-4, as can be seen in the change in stonework to the right of the two windows. It is now a Greek Orthodox church dedicated to St Andrew.

▼ Torquay, Tormohun Church interior 1889 21474

The interior contains many monuments to the Cary family of Torre Abbey, covering four centuries: there is a brass to Wilmota (died 1581), wife of George Cary; the tomb of George Cary (died 1758), who 'for his Religious and Charitable disposition was esteemed in life and lamented in death'; and one of the peal of six bells hung in 1911 was given by Col Lucius Cary in memory of the many Carys buried here.

▲ Torquay St Marychurch 1920 69605

St Mary's is reputed to be the oldest church site in Devon. The church was rebuilt in 1861 and the tower went up in 1873 at a cost of £3,500 in memory of Bishop Philpott, who is buried in the churchyard. An attack by a lone German bomber on 30 April 1943 killed 26 people, most of whom were children. The church was rebuilt in 1952-6.

Torquay St Mary's Church Interior 1889 21515

The Norman font was discovered in 1824 to be upside-down. The carved portion had been buried to hide it from the Puritans and an octagonal top placed on the upturned bottom. Now restored to its correct orientation, there has been some debate as to the nature of its carvings, including one argument about whether one figure is a beaver or a wild ass!

St Marychurch, St Denis Porch and Priory 1894 33665
Until the mid-19th century Torquay's Catholics worshipped at the private chapel of the Cary family at Torre Abbey. Then in 1860-70 the Church of Our Lady Help of Christians and St Denis was built. The air raid that destroyed St Mary's also made its mark here, dislodging the top stone of the spire.

St Marychurch, Church of Our Lady and St Denis Interior 1927 79712
The building of Our Lady Help of Christians and St Denis is a good example of Victorian philanthropy: the sole benefactor for this big project was William John Potts Chatto of the Daison, who is buried in the Lady Chapel.

Torquay, Holy Trinity Church 1899 44561
Built in 1896 in the Gothic style, Holy Trinity replaced an old independent chapel and eventually came under the Church of England. The building was sold in 1980 and became the Breakaway sports centre in 1982.

Ipplepen, St Andrew's Church c1960 127009
The 91-foot tower of St Andrew's was built in 1440 and is unusual for a Devon church in that it has eight pinnacles. The rest of the church was rebuilt in the 15th century and has a beautifully carved oak pulpit and a fine Perpendicular rood screen.

Abbotskerswell, Church of the Virgin Mary, Interior 1890 25461
The Church of the Virgin Mary was originally a cell of the Priory of Montacute near Yeovil, and later belonged to the Abbot of Sherborne until the dissolution. The church was built in the 13th and 15th centuries and restored in 1884.

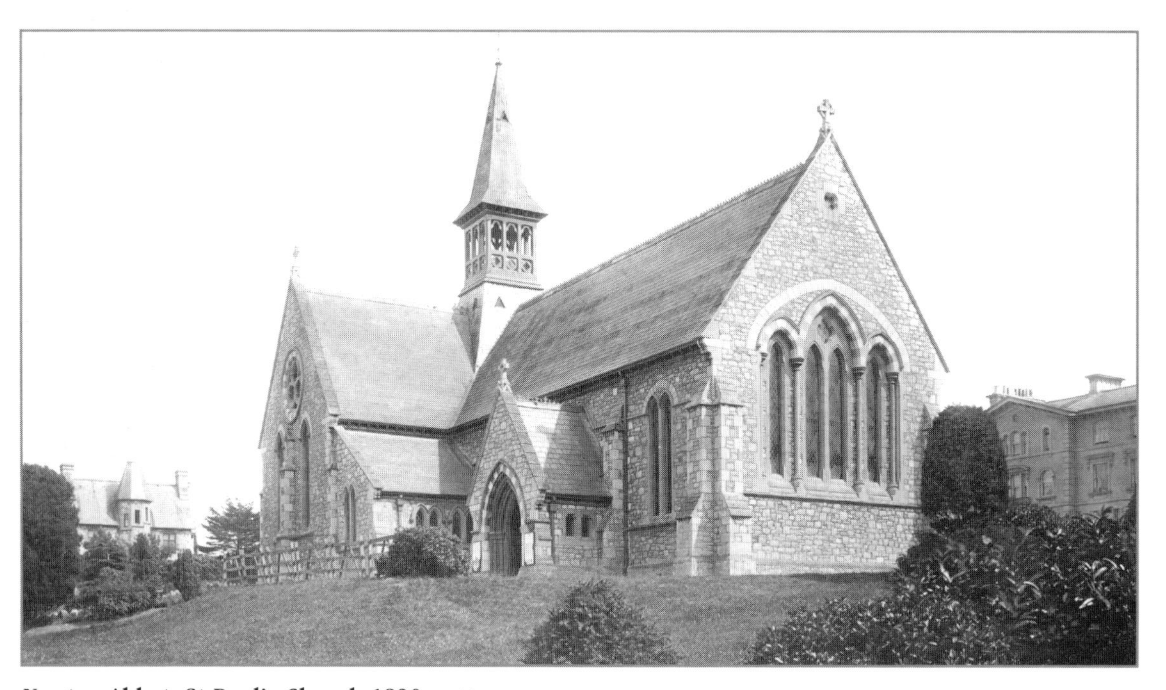

Newton Abbot, St Paul's Church 1890 25460
St Paul's was built in the Early English style by the Earl of Devon in 1861. The font was donated by the Bishop of Exeter and the lectern by local railway workers. It was damaged in a German bombing raid in May 1942 and subsequently renovated.

Newton Abbot, Highweek Church 1890 25456
Standing above the valley of the River Lemon, All Saints was built in 1428 by Richard Yarde of Bradley Manor. There had previously been a chapel of ease on the site. Like many other Devon churches it was restored in Victorian times.

▼ Newton Abbot, St Leonard's Church 1896 38202

The original St Leonard's dates back to about 1220 and the tower still stands in the centre of town. This, the replacement for the old church, was built on the site of the old parsonage, the £2,500 cost being raised by public subscription. It was consecrated by Bishop Philpotts on 24 November 1836.

▼ Teignmouth, The Roman Catholic Church 1906 56568

Teignmouth's Catholics used to celebrate Mass in a room at the Jolly Sailor pub, hired by Fr Charles Lomax. Then in 1854 the Church of St Charles was built, designed by the Hansom brothers, who also designed Plymouth Cathedral.

▲ Teignmouth Roman Catholic Church Interior 1907 58127

In 1884 the railway tunnel over which the church stood was demolished. St Charles was pulled down and transported to Plymouth to be re-erected as Holy Cross. The present church of Our Lady and St Patrick (see also photograph 56568) was built at the expense of the railway company.

◄ **Teignmouth Congregational Church Interior 1907** 58126
One of the earliest non-conformist churches in Teignmouth, Zion Chapel, was built on this site in Dawlish Street in 1790. It was demolished in 1883 and the present building erected at a cost of £3,700. It is now the United Reformed Church.

Shaldon, St Peter's Church 1906 54072
St Peter's was built in 1893-4 on a site near Shaldon Bridge which had been bought by the Rev R M Marsh-Dunn. Built from the local red sandstone, it was completed in 1902 and consecrated by Bishop Ryle.

Shaldon, St Peter's Church interior 1903 49569
The interior of St Peter's has piers and dressings of polyphant stone and a marble pulpit with alabaster steps. The figures on the beautiful carved stone rood screen are (left to right): St John, St Paul, St Peter, the Blessed Virgin Mary and St Nicholas.

Kenton, All Saints Church, The Pulpit and Screen 1907 58177

The magnificent screen, extending the width of the church, was erected in 1478-86 as a gift of Bishop Courtenay. It may have been carved by Flemish carvers. The pulpit was restored from drawings made by Rev Sabine Baring-Gould when he was a boy. All Saints was built in 1370, and the tower and porch added in the reign of Henry IV.

Bishopsteignton, St John's Church 1890 26050
St John the Baptist was built in 1130 on the site of an old Saxon church. The north aisle was added in the 15th century, and in 1815 the tower and turret were demolished and the stone used to build the present tower. A spire was added, but removed in 1869 when 'the tower was raised and the present parapet, pinnacles, gargoyles and other decorations added in the most florid Gothic possible.'

Bishopsteignton, St John's Church Interior 1890 26051
The east window, presented by Rev G S Hele in the 19th century, shows St John the Baptist, the emblems of the four evangelists, and twelve small scenes depicting portions of the litany. Over the old south doorway is one of the finest tympanums in Devon, the only one to show the adoration of the Magi.

East Devon

Membury
St John's Church and Schools 1902 48478
The 13th-century church of St John the Baptist stands in an area that has been occupied since Roman times. The south chapel contains several monuments to the Frys of nearby Yarty, including Nick Fry, Sheriff of Devon, who died in 1632.

Kilmington
St Giles' Church 1902

48471

The church of St Giles was originally built in the 14th and 15th centuries, but was largely rebuilt in 1862 by C F Edwards. The tower is all that remains of the old church, along with 18th-century monuments to Thomas Southcott and Agnes Tucker of Coryton.

▼ **Rousdon, The Church 1900** 46054
Sir Henry Williamson Peek, of the biscuit family, built a mansion here in 1870 and while he was at it got his architects, George and Vaughan, to build this church. The Devon historian Hoskins, who seems not to have been a fan of Victorian church building, said 'It has nothing to recommend it.'

▼ **Colyton, St Andrew's Church 1907** 58037
There is thought to have been a Saxon church on this site before AD700, and the Norman structure, dedicated to St Andrew, is built on Saxon foundations. The unusual octagonal lantern was installed in the 15th century when Colyton was one of the three richest wool towns in Devon. The clock was made in 1710 by Lewis Pridham of Crediton. The north aisle was enlarged in 1888.

▲ **Seaton Church of St Gregory 1898** 42426
The Church of St Gregory was built in the early 14th century and the west tower added in the 15th. It was extensively restored in 1866 when one of the arcades was removed, giving the interior its unusual appearance.

Beer
St Michael's Church
1903 49602

This was originally the site of the old chapel of ease for St Gregory's in Seaton. The chapel was demolished in 1875 and construction of St Michael's commenced in 1876. The spire has since been taken down because it was unsafe.

Sidmouth Church of St Giles and St Nicholas, and War Memorial 1924 76373
The first vicar took up his living here in 1175, around the time the church was first built. It was completely rebuilt in 1450, and restored in 1859. The church is dedicated to St Nicholas, patron saint of sailors, and St Giles, who was much revered by the monks of Mont Saint Michel in Normandy, one time owners of the manor of Sidmouth.

Salcomb Regis St Peter's Church 1928 81059

The earliest mention of this Norman church is 1149, although during the reign of King Athelstan (AD925-940) there was a wooden church here. The tower was built by Bishop Lacy in 1450 with stone quarried from a hillside nearby, and only then did the church receive its present dedication to St Peter - previously it had been dedicated to the Blessed Virgin Mary.

Sidmouth Church Chapel 1928 81054A

The Lady Chapel Window contains a rare 15th-century fragment of glass known as the 'Five Wounds Window', depicting the wounds of Christ. The west window was given by Queen Victoria in memory of her father the Duke of Kent, who died in Sidmouth in 1820. The window was designed in 1867 by Hughes and depicts some of St Nicholas' deeds.

Sidmouth All Saints Church 1906 53806

All Saints was built in 1837 on land donated by Sir John Kennaway. Construction cost £3,000 of which £1,500 was given by Rev Joseph Bradney. In 1869 Rev Baring Baring Gould became vicar; he was one of the enormous tribe of Baring Goulds, of whom the most famous was Sabine Baring Gould of Lew Trenchard.

Upottery, Church of St Mary c1960 U28003

The Church of St Mary at Upottery is mainly a 13th- and 14th-century structure, but with the odd hint of Norman. The tower and font are both 15th-century and the aisle and chapel were rebuilt in 1875. The church contains monuments to the Addington family, once owners of the local manor. Henry Addington became Prime Minister in 1801 and took the title of Viscount.

Ottery St Mary, St Mary's Church 1901 47848

One of Devon's finest churches, St Mary's was modelled on Exeter Cathedral by Bishop Grandison, who started rebuilding in 1342, not long after he had gained the church from the canons of Rouen. It is one of just seventeen churches in Simon Jenkins' 'England's Thousand Best Churches' to receive five stars. Enough said!

Newton Poppleford, The Village and St Luke's Church 1906

53835

St Luke's started life in the 14th century as a chantry chapel and in 1331 became a chapel of ease for travellers to Aylesbeare church some four miles off. Only the tower and porch remain of the original structure; the rest was rebuilt in 1826 when the south aisle was added, and further rebuilding occurred in 1875 and 1897.

◄ **Otterton**
The Church Interior
1907 58188

In 1066 William the Conqueror granted land here to the monks of Mont Saint Michel, who built a Benedictine priory. The priory was suppressed in 1414, and the 13th-century tower is the only remnant. In 1869-71 the nave and aisles were built by Benjamin Ferry for the Rolles, one of the richest and most powerful Devon families.

▼ **Budleigh Salterton, St Peter's Church 1895** 36062
Budleigh Salterton was originally served by the Rolle Chapel which was built in 1813 on Chapel Street. St Peter's was built in 1893-4 for the Hon Mark Rolle by G H Fellows-Prynne. The Rolles were major benefactors of the town who also donated the cemetery.

▼ **Rockbeare, St Mary's Church c1960** r257009
St Mary's was rebuilt in 1887-9, and only the tower, the west door, part of the north aisle wall and the Elizabethan parapet of the west gallery remain of the original church. Hoskins refers to it as 'A melancholy exhibition of "restoration"'.

▲ **Woodbury, St Swithin's Church 1906** 53996
There may have been a Saxon church on the site of St Swithin's as early as the 7th century, but the present church dates from 1409 (the tower) and the 1530s. In the 19th century St Swithin's underwent a fifty-year restoration by one of those improbably long-lived Victorian vicars, Rev J Loveband Fulford, who (amongst other things) took out a carved medieval rood screen so his parishioners could hear him better.

Topsham St Margaret's Church from the River Exe c1965 T59003
The medieval red sandstone tower of St Margaret's is rather dwarfed by the main body of the church, built in 1874-6 by Edward Ashworth. The font is Norman, and the church's roots go back even further - in AD937 King Athelstan gave the site to the monastery of St Mary and St Peter at Exeter.

Central Devon

Holcombe Rogus, All Saints Church c1960
H243037
The 15th-century structure of All Saints is strongly associated with the Bluett family of nearby Holcombe Court, which was built by Sir Roger Bluett in the early 16th century and stayed in the family until 1858. The 17th-century Bluett pew can be seen at the end of the north aisle and there are memorials to several family members including Rev Robert Bluett, who died in 1749.

Tiverton, Blundell's School Chapel 1930 83218
Blundell's School was founded in 1599 by Tiverton merchant Peter Blundell. The school occupied the same site from 1604 until 1880, when it moved to bigger premises. The school had never had a chapel before, but pressure from assistant master Rev T U Cross led to one being built in 1883.

Tiverton, Blundell's School Chapel, interior 1930 83219
Among the old boys of Blundell's are Jack Russell, the famous hunting parson of Swimbridge, Archbishop Temple, and the author R D Blackmore, who was sufficiently impressed to send his most famous character here - John Ridd, hero of Lorna Doone.

Exeter, The Cathedral, South-East View 1887 19603
Bishop Warlewast built the Norman towers of the Cathedral of St Peter in the 12th century, and these were incorporated as transepts into the Gothic cathedral built in the early 14th century. Most cathedrals have their towers at the west front, but in Exeter's case this is occupied by a magnificent three-tiered sculptured screen.

Exeter, The Cathedral, Nave East 1896 37998
The ribbed vaulting of the 300-foot nave is unique in England. It was completed by Bishop Grandison and rests on blue-grey columns of Purbeck marble. On either side of the golden gates in the Great Screen are altars to Blessed Mary and St Nicholas. The organ above was built in 1665.

Newton St Cyres, Church of St Cyriac and St Julietta c1955 n83020
The Church of St Cyriac and St Julietta was built at the beginning of the 14th century from red Posbury stone. Inside, the monument to John Northcote of Hayne (1632) is unusually lavish - Devon carvers, working in isolation and with little influence from outside the county, tended to be very conservative.

Tedburn St Mary, The Village and St Mary's Church c1960 T151017
The oldest parts of St Mary's are 13th- and 14th-century, found in the south transept and north arcade. The tower is 15th century and the chancel was rebuilt by John Ashworth in 1868. Outside is a fine sundial erected in 1817 by the churchwardens Edward Osmond and John Francis.

Cheriton Fitzpaine, St Matthew's Church c1960 C305005
This may well have been an ancient site of worship, as Cheriton is the Saxon for 'Church Town'. St Matthew's was built in the 15th century from Beer stone, with piers modelled on those of Exeter Cathedral. It was restored in 1883-5 by James Crocker.

▼ **Sandford, St Swithin's Church c1955** S759013
St Swithin's was originally built as a chapel of ease for travellers to Holy Cross at Crediton in 1523-4. There are several monuments to the Davie family, who occupied nearby Creedy Park from 1627-1846, and the west gallery was erected by Sir John Davie in 1675. The church was restored, and the clerestory added in 1847-8.

▼ **Down St Mary, Church of St Mary c1955** D247005
The remote Church of St Mary started life as a 12th-century building at a crossroads. The tower was built in 1413 to replace one destroyed in a hurricane, and the rest of the church was rebuilt in 1871 during the incumbency of Rev R T A Radford. It has fine 16th-century carved bench-ends.

▲ **Okehampton Fore Street and St James's Chapel 1929** 52490
Founded in 1178 by the Norman Reginald de Courtenay as a chapel of ease, St James's Chapel was rebuilt in 1382. By the late 18th century it had fallen into disrepair and came within a hair's breadth of being condemned in 1851 before being restored by Edward Ashworth in 1862.

Okehampton The Wesleyan Chapel 1906 56050

This church was built at Fairplace in 1904 to replace the original one in New Road which had stood since 1842. Now the Okehampton United Church, shared by Methodists and the United Reformed Church, Fairplace church was closed for renovation in September 1963 and rededicated on 13 May 1964.

Northlew, St Thomas of Canterbury Church c1960 N85014
The church here dates from around the time of the first rector, Richard de Boleville, in 1258. All that remains of the original structure is the base of the tower, the west door and north and south windows. The present church is 15th-century and was restored in 1537 and 1885.

Northlew, St Thomas of Canterbury Church Interior c1960 N85015
The pews date from the 1537 restoration, as does the barrel roof of the north aisle, which contains some very fine floral, leaf and face bosses. The screen is 15th-century and was restored in the 19th century by Herbert Reed. The font originated in 1150 and was reassembled from fragments in 1870.

Broadwoodwidger, St Nicholas' Church c1950 B388301
Standing above the valley of the River Wolf, the Church of St Nicholas is first recorded in 1288 when a Parochial Quota of £13 was paid to the Deanery of Tavistock. The chancel arch and font date from this time, the tower is late 14th-century and the south aisle was added during a restoration of 1531. In 1965 the nave roof succumbed to the ravages of Death Watch Beetle and collapsed, necessitating the raising of £10,000 for repairs.

North Devon

Holsworthy, Church of St Peter and St Paul c1955 H161017
The earliest part of the Church of St Peter and St Paul is the Norman south doorway. The tower was built in 1450, onto a nave that dates from the 13th and 14th centuries. In 1884 Rev G W Thornton added the north aisle and rebuilt the chancel. An unusual custom is the 'Pretty Maids' Charity', under which income from a legacy is paid annually 'to the young single woman resident in Holsworthy who is generally esteemed by the young as the most deserving, the most handsome, and the most noted for her quietness and attendance at church.'

Clovelly, All Saints Church 1906 55958
All Saints was built in the 15th and 16th centuries on the site of a Norman Church which, in turn, had been built on the site of a Saxon church. The church has many monuments to the seven generations of Carys who lived at Clovelly Court from 1457-1740. William Cary, who donated the pulpit in 1634, was the model for Will Cary in Charles Kingsley's Westward Ho!

Parkham, The Village and St James's Church c1955 P161005
St James has a fine late-Norman south doorway and font. The rest of the church is 15th-century with early 16th-century aisles - the north one was built by the Risdons of Bableigh, and the south by the Giffards of Halsbury. The arcades are of Lundy granite; brought down from the top of Lundy island, the stone underwent a fifteen mile passage by sea before the masons could use it.

◄ **Northam, St Margaret's Church 1919** 69346
The conspicuous tower of St Margaret's has long been used as a landmark by mariners negotiating Bideford Bar at the entrance to the Torridge estuary. Until 1844 the tower was rendered and whitewashed to make it more visible, but Rev J H Gosset removed the rendering during his restoration, which presumably did little to endear him to the maritime portion of his flock.

◄ **Abbotsham Church of St Helen South Side 1890** 24838
As its name suggests, Abbotsham was part of the endowment of Tavistock in the 10th century. The Church of St Helen dates from the 13th century and has fine 16th-century carved bench ends showing the crucifixion, Christ carrying the cross, saints, a tumbler, ornamental initials, medallions and leaves.

▼ **Northam, The Church 1890** 24833
According to an inscription on one of the octagonal piers, the north aisle was built in 1593, although a church must have existed here much earlier as the font is 13th-century. The chancel was rebuilt in 1865.

◄ **Torrington St Michael's Church Interior 1923** 75108
In 1645 St Michael's suffered an unusual fate for a church. Following Fairfax's rout of the royalist forces under Sir Ralph Hopton, the church was being used as a magazine and prison. Whether by accident or design is unclear, but 80 barrels of gunpowder exploded, taking around 200 men into the hereafter. The church was rebuilt in 1651 and the tower and spire added in 1828.

◄ **Weare Giffard Church of the Holy Trinity 1890** 24855
The nave and chancel of Holy Trinity are 14th-century and the south aisle and tower a century or so younger. The oldest parts of the church are glass fragments on some of the windows that may be as old as 1300, and there is a wall painting of St Sebastian meeting his end at the hands of the archers.

◄ **Weare Giffard, Church of the Holy Trinity 1923** 75117
The Church of the Holy Trinity stands next to the manor house of the Fortescue family, built in 1454. The fine 15th-century chancel roof may well have been built by the same carpenter who built the magnificent hammer beam roof of the Great Hall in the manor house. The Fortescues' connection with the church is commemorated in a 1638 wall monument to four generations of the family.

▼ **Bideford St Peter's Church 1907** 59283
The growing Victorian population of East-the-Water's first place of worship was a prefabricated 'iron church' built in 1881. It was replaced by St Peter's, designed by R T Hookway and consecrated by the Bishop of Exeter on 28 June 1890.

◄ **Fremington St Paul's Church c1955** f100001
The Church of St Paul has a 15th-century stone pulpit and an Elizabethan communion table. It was restored in 1866-7 by Sir George Gilbert Scott, the populariser of High Victorian Gothic who also designed the Albert Memorial and St Pancras Station.

Barnstaple, St Mary's Church Interior 1919 69316
St Mary Magdalene was built in 1844-6 by Benjamin Ferrey, one of many Victorian architects kept in work designing churches to accommodate a rapidly-expanding population. Such was the demand that architects worked all over the country; Ferrey is best known for his work on Christ Church, Kennington and Roehampton Old Church.

Barnstaple, St Peter's Church 1919 69319
St Peter's was consecrated in 1318 by Bishop Stapleton. Its unusual lead-covered octagonal broach spire was erected in 1389 and, despite restoration in the 17th century, is now slightly twisted. 17th-century decorated floor tiles, made in Barnstaple, can still be seen around the pulpit.

Tawstock, St Peter's Church 1890 24882
The 14th-century Church of St Peter looks out over the valley of the River Taw and is unusual for a Devon church in that it is cruciform in shape, with the tower above the crossing of transept and nave. Inside are monuments to the Bourchier and Wrey families, owners of Tawstock Court up the valley.

Pilton, St Mary's Church and Old Village c1955 P52008
St Mary's was originally part of a Benedictine Priory, one of several founded by King Athelstan. The priory went the same way as many others at the dissolution of the monasteries in 1533 but St Mary's, dedicated by Bishop Bronescombe in 1259, was spared.

Pilton, St Mary's Church, Chancel 1900 45723
The church contains several monuments to the Chichester family of Raleigh, the oldest being that to Richard Chichester, who died in 1493. Others include Sir John Chichester (d 1569), twice Sheriff of Devon, and Sir Robert Chichester, who died in 1627 as a result of a fall from his horse on Pilton Bridge. The fate of the horse is not known.

Shirwell, St Peter's Church c1955 S357029

St Peter's was built, like so many churches, in stages; the nave was completed in the 13th century, the chancel in the 14th and the south aisle in the 15th. It contains monuments to the branch of the Chichester family who lived at nearby Youlston Park and whose most famous son - the aviator and yachtsman Sir Francis Chichester - is buried next to the porch.

Swimbridge, St James's Church Interior 1900 45725

The pulpit here at St James was used for forty six years in the 19th century by Jack Russell, the famous hunting parson. His sermons were by Victorian standards blessedly brief, on account of his hunting horse usually being saddled and waiting in the churchyard. His biggest claim to fame, however, is the breeding of the terrier named after him and which also gives the name of the local pub.

Landkey St Paul's Church c1855 l193301
Although the 15th-century church is dedicated to St Paul, Landkey itself takes its name from St Kea, a 6th-century missionary from Glastonbury. The south transept of St Paul's is the Acland chapel, named after the Aclands who held Acland Barton from the 12th century right into the 20th.

South Molton, Church of St Mary Magdalene c1900 S362301
St Mary Magdalene is the third church to stand on this site. Details of the first are lost in the mists of time, but the second was built in the 12th and 13th centuries. The current tower dates from 1435 and the rest of the church from the late 15th century. Until 1751 the 102-foot tower was topped by a spire, but this was struck by lightning and damaged so badly it had to be removed.

Filleigh, St Paul's Church c1955 F99007
There was once a Celtic chapel on or near this site, dedicated to St Fili, travelling companion of St Kea, but the present church is dedicated to St Paul. The medieval tower and nave walls survive, but the rest was rebuilt by the Fortescues in 1732 and rebuilt again in 1876-7.

Saunton, St Ann's Church and Vicarage 1912 64537
St Ann's chapel was known as the 'Chapel in the Sands' and measured a mere 14 feet 6 inches by 12 feet. It stood in the dunes near the lighthouse at the northern side of the crossing of the Torridge estuary from Appledore. The chapel fell into disrepair and is now gone; this is a modern chapel of ease.

Georgeham, St George's Church c1960 G323026
The 14th-century tower and a piscina in the chancel are all that remain of the old church after its rebuilding by James Fower in 1876-7 for the Hole family. St George's does retain some old artefacts - a panel of the crucifixion from about 1300, and in the south chapel an effigy of Mauger of St Aubyn, who died in 1294.

Mortehoe, Church of St Mary Magdalene 1935 87130

The 13th-century Church of St Mary Magdalene, founded by a priest named William de Tracey, stands opposite the local pub, named the Ship Aground in memory of the many ships that met their end on nearby Morte Point. The close proximity of church and pub is common in rural parishes, giving worshippers the chance of refreshment before the long walk back home.

Mortehoe, Church of St Mary Magdalene, Interior 1935 87131

The enormous mosaic above the chancel arch was created in 1905 in memory of the churchwarden's wife. The churchwarden in question must have been a wealthy man, for the mosaic was designed by the Oxford Professor of Art Selwyn Image and made by the same craftsmen responsible for the mosaics in St Paul's Cathedral.

Parracombe The Old Church of St Petrock's 1907

59443

Parracombe's original church stands on the site of St Petrock's church, which was the earliest Christian church in Devon, having been founded in the 6th century. This 16th-century church, now used only occasionally, has an almost unspoilt Georgian interior.

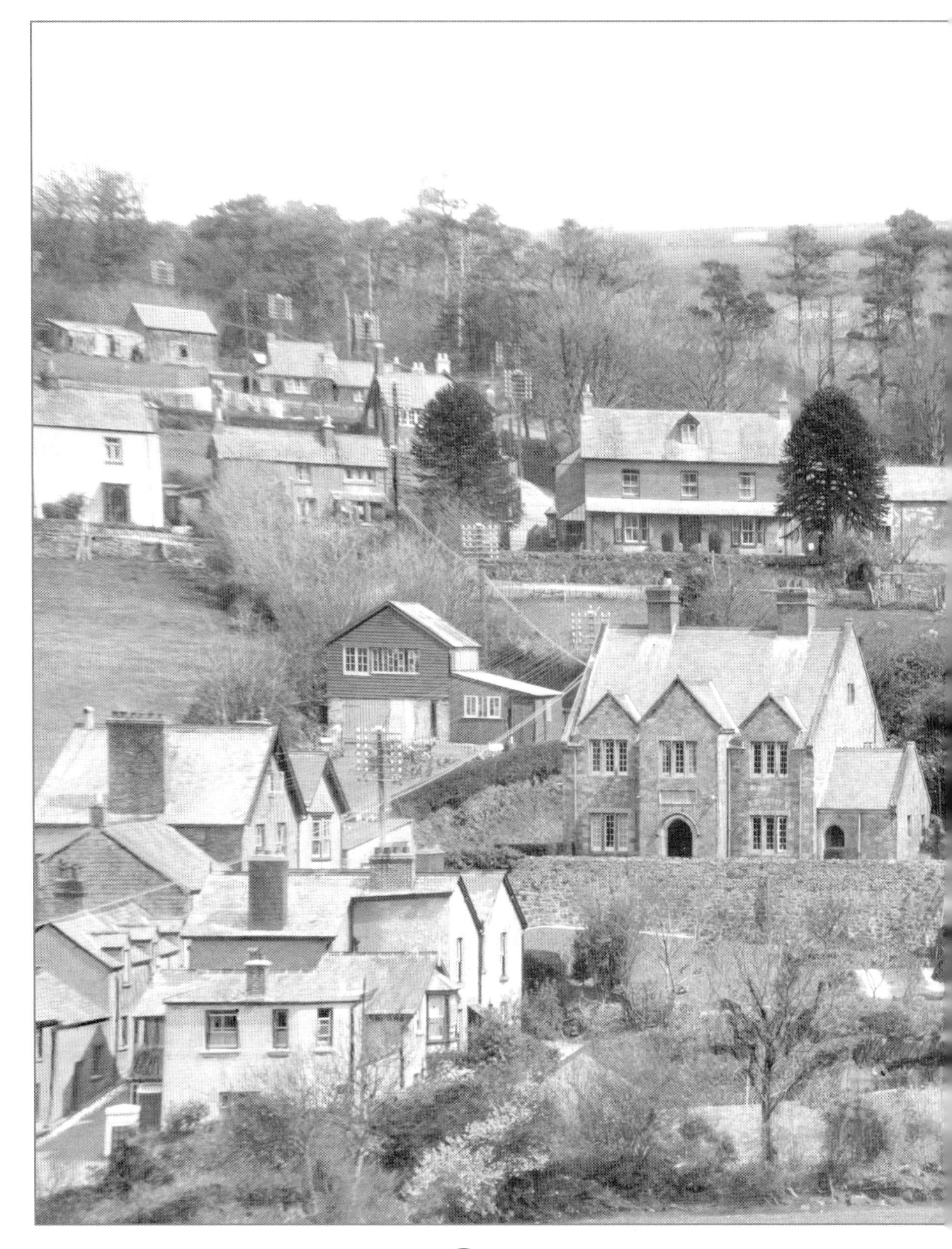

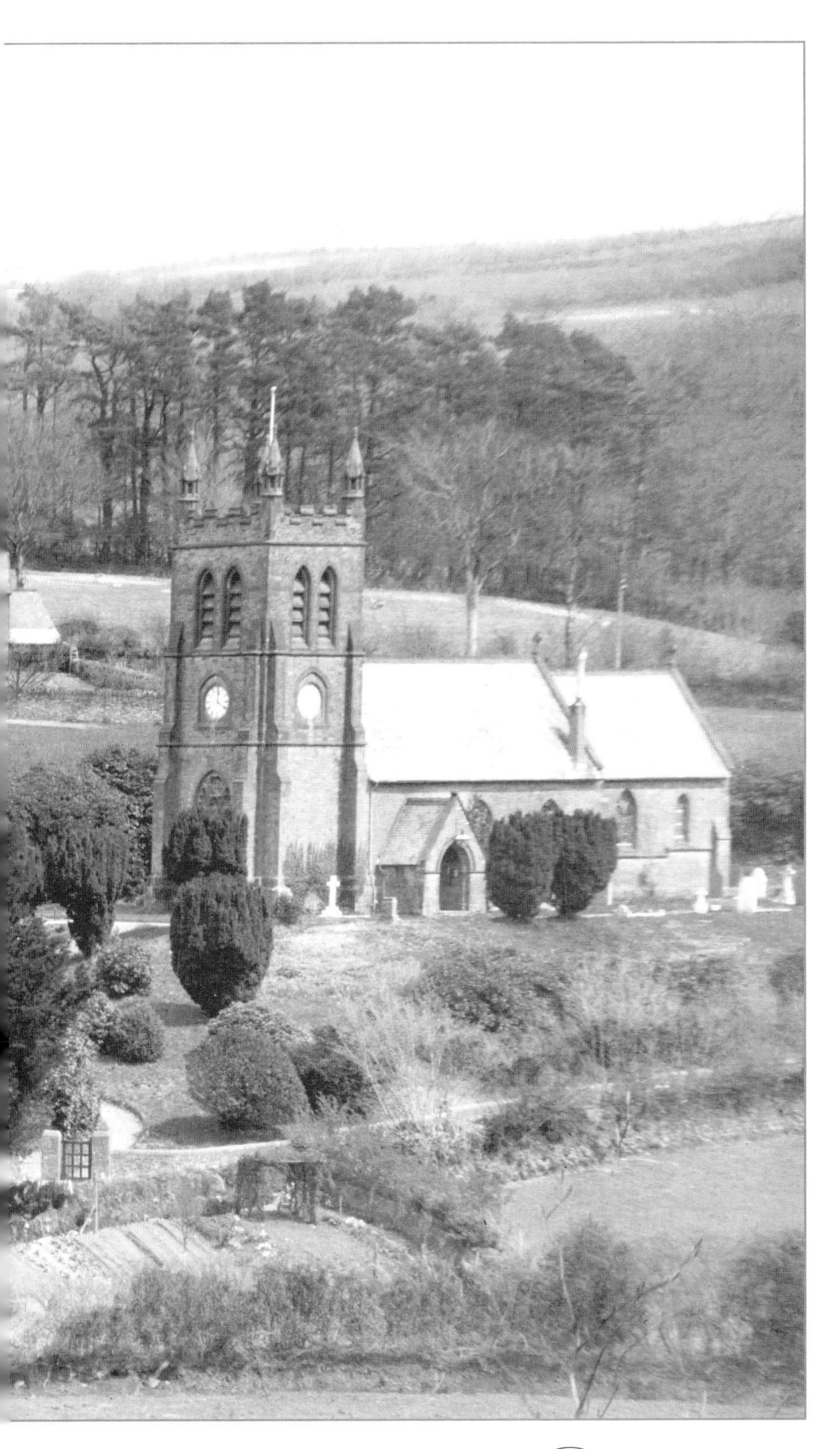

Parracombe The Church and Schools c1955 P11003
Parracombe's newer church stands in the village (the old one is a little way off) and was built in the 19th century. Plans to demolish the old church were abandoned following a campaign in 1879, led by the critic and writer John Ruskin. Consequently Parracombe now has two churches.

Lynton, St Mary's Church c1965 l127073
St Mary's has a 13th-century tower and a Norman font. The nave was rebuilt in 1741 and the north aisle added in 1817. The church underwent a series of Victorian and Edwardian restorations and rebuildings in 1868-9, 1893-5 and 1905.

Countisbury, St John's Church 1907 59407
St John the Baptist stands high above the Bristol Channel on windswept Countisbury Common. The only remnant of the original medieval church is a carved bench end with a crowned swan and arms. The nave was rebuilt in 1716, the tower in 1835, and the arcade in 1846.

Index

Frith Book Co Titles

www.francisfrith.co.uk

The Frith Book Company publishes over 100 new titles each year. A selection of those currently available are listed below. For latest catalogue please contact Frith Book Co.

Town Books 96 pages, approx 100 photos. County and Themed Books 128 pages, approx 150 photos (unless specified). All titles hardback laminated case and jacket except those indicated pb (paperback)

Title	ISBN	Price
Amersham, Chesham & Rickmansworth (pb)	1-85937-340-2	£9.99
Ancient Monuments & Stone Circles	1-85937-143-4	£17.99
Aylesbury (pb)	1-85937-227-9	£9.99
Bakewell	1-85937-113-2	£12.99
Barnstaple (pb)	1-85937-300-3	£9.99
Bath (pb)	1-85937419-0	£9.99
Bedford (pb)	1-85937-205-8	£9.99
Berkshire (pb)	1-85937-191-4	£9.99
Berkshire Churches	1-85937-170-1	£17.99
Blackpool (pb)	1-85937-382-8	£9.99
Bognor Regis (pb)	1-85937-431-x	£9.99
Bournemouth	1-85937-067-5	£12.99
Bradford (pb)	1-85937-204-x	£9.99
Brighton & Hove(pb)	1-85937-192-2	£8.99
Bristol (pb)	1-85937-264-3	£9.99
British Life A Century Ago (pb)	1-85937-213-9	£9.99
Buckinghamshire (pb)	1-85937-200-7	£9.99
Camberley (pb)	1-85937-222-8	£9.99
Cambridge (pb)	1-85937-422-0	£9.99
Cambridgeshire (pb)	1-85937-420-4	£9.99
Canals & Waterways (pb)	1-85937-291-0	£9.99
Canterbury Cathedral (pb)	1-85937-179-5	£9.99
Cardiff (pb)	1-85937-093-4	£9.99
Carmarthenshire	1-85937-216-3	£14.99
Chelmsford (pb)	1-85937-310-0	£9.99
Cheltenham (pb)	1-85937-095-0	£9.99
Cheshire (pb)	1-85937-271-6	£9.99
Chester	1-85937-090-x	£12.99
Chesterfield	1-85937-378-x	£9.99
Chichester (pb)	1-85937-228-7	£9.99
Colchester (pb)	1-85937-188-4	£8.99
Cornish Coast	1-85937-163-9	£14.99
Cornwall (pb)	1-85937-229-5	£9.99
Cornwall Living Memories	1-85937-248-1	£14.99
Cotswolds (pb)	1-85937-230-9	£9.99
Cotswolds Living Memories	1-85937-255-4	£14.99
County Durham	1-85937-123-x	£14.99
Croydon Living Memories	1-85937-162-0	£9.99
Cumbria	1-85937-101-9	£14.99
Dartmoor	1-85937-145-0	£14.99
Derby (pb)	1-85937-367-4	£9.99
Derbyshire (pb)	1-85937-196-5	£9.99
Devon (pb)	1-85937-297-x	£9.99
Dorset (pb)	1-85937-269-4	£9.99
Dorset Churches	1-85937-172-8	£17.99
Dorset Coast (pb)	1-85937-299-6	£9.99
Dorset Living Memories	1-85937-210-4	£14.99
Down the Severn	1-85937-118-3	£14.99
Down the Thames (pb)	1-85937-278-3	£9.99
Down the Trent	1-85937-311-9	£14.99
Dublin (pb)	1-85937-231-7	£9.99
East Anglia (pb)	1-85937-265-1	£9.99
East London	1-85937-080-2	£14.99
East Sussex	1-85937-130-2	£14.99
Eastbourne	1-85937-061-6	£12.99
Edinburgh (pb)	1-85937-193-0	£8.99
England in the 1880s	1-85937-331-3	£17.99
English Castles (pb)	1-85937-434-4	£9.99
English Country Houses	1-85937-161-2	£17.99
Essex (pb)	1-85937-270-8	£9.99
Exeter	1-85937-126-4	£12.99
Exmoor	1-85937-132-9	£14.99
Falmouth	1-85937-066-7	£12.99
Folkestone (pb)	1-85937-124-8	£9.99
Glasgow (pb)	1-85937-190-6	£9.99
Gloucestershire	1-85937-102-7	£14.99
Great Yarmouth (pb)	1-85937-426-3	£9.99
Greater Manchester (pb)	1-85937-266-x	£9.99
Guildford (pb)	1-85937-410-7	£9.99
Hampshire (pb)	1-85937-279-1	£9.99
Hampshire Churches (pb)	1-85937-207-4	£9.99
Harrogate	1-85937-423-9	£9.99
Hastings & Bexhill (pb)	1-85937-131-0	£9.99
Heart of Lancashire (pb)	1-85937-197-3	£9.99
Helston (pb)	1-85937-214-7	£9.99
Hereford (pb)	1-85937-175-2	£9.99
Herefordshire	1-85937-174-4	£14.99
Hertfordshire (pb)	1-85937-247-3	£9.99
Horsham (pb)	1-85937-432-8	£9.99
Humberside	1-85937-215-5	£14.99
Hythe, Romney Marsh & Ashford	1-85937-256-2	£9.99

Available from your local bookshop or from the publisher

Frith Book Co Titles (continued)

Title	ISBN	Price
Ipswich (pb)	1-85937-424-7	£9.99
Ireland (pb)	1-85937-181-7	£9.99
Isle of Man (pb)	1-85937-268-6	£9.99
Isles of Scilly	1-85937-136-1	£14.99
Isle of Wight (pb)	1-85937-429-8	£9.99
Isle of Wight Living Memories	1-85937-304-6	£14.99
Kent (pb)	1-85937-189-2	£9.99
Kent Living Memories	1-85937-125-6	£14.99
Lake District (pb)	1-85937-275-9	£9.99
Lancaster, Morecambe & Heysham (pb)	1-85937-233-3	£9.99
Leeds (pb)	1-85937-202-3	£9.99
Leicester	1-85937-073-x	£12.99
Leicestershire (pb)	1-85937-185-x	£9.99
Lincolnshire (pb)	1-85937-433-6	£9.99
Liverpool & Merseyside (pb)	1-85937-234-1	£9.99
London (pb)	1-85937-183-3	£9.99
Ludlow (pb)	1-85937-176-0	£9.99
Luton (pb)	1-85937-235-x	£9.99
Maidstone	1-85937-056-x	£14.99
Manchester (pb)	1-85937-198-1	£9.99
Middlesex	1-85937-158-2	£14.99
New Forest	1-85937-128-0	£14.99
Newark (pb)	1-85937-366-6	£9.99
Newport, Wales (pb)	1-85937-258-9	£9.99
Newquay (pb)	1-85937-421-2	£9.99
Norfolk (pb)	1-85937-195-7	£9.99
Norfolk Living Memories	1-85937-217-1	£14.99
Northamptonshire	1-85937-150-7	£14.99
Northumberland Tyne & Wear (pb)	1-85937-281-3	£9.99
North Devon Coast	1-85937-146-9	£14.99
North Devon Living Memories	1-85937-261-9	£14.99
North London	1-85937-206-6	£14.99
North Wales (pb)	1-85937-298-8	£9.99
North Yorkshire (pb)	1-85937-236-8	£9.99
Norwich (pb)	1-85937-194-9	£8.99
Nottingham (pb)	1-85937-324-0	£9.99
Nottinghamshire (pb)	1-85937-187-6	£9.99
Oxford (pb)	1-85937-411-5	£9.99
Oxfordshire (pb)	1-85937-430-1	£9.99
Peak District (pb)	1-85937-280-5	£9.99
Penzance	1-85937-069-1	£12.99
Peterborough (pb)	1-85937-219-8	£9.99
Piers	1-85937-237-6	£17.99
Plymouth	1-85937-119-1	£12.99
Poole & Sandbanks (pb)	1-85937-251-1	£9.99
Preston (pb)	1-85937-212-0	£9.99
Reading (pb)	1-85937-238-4	£9.99
Romford (pb)	1-85937-319-4	£9.99
Salisbury (pb)	1-85937-239-2	£9.99
Scarborough (pb)	1-85937-379-8	£9.99
St Albans (pb)	1-85937-341-0	£9.99

Title	ISBN	Price
St Ives (pb)	1-85937415-8	£9.99
Scotland (pb)	1-85937-182-5	£9.99
Scottish Castles (pb)	1-85937-323-2	£9.99
Sevenoaks & Tunbridge	1-85937-057-8	£12.99
Sheffield, South Yorks (pb)	1-85937-267-8	£9.99
Shrewsbury (pb)	1-85937-325-9	£9.99
Shropshire (pb)	1-85937-326-7	£9.99
Somerset	1-85937-153-1	£14.99
South Devon Coast	1-85937-107-8	£14.99
South Devon Living Memories	1-85937-168-x	£14.99
South Hams	1-85937-220-1	£14.99
Southampton (pb)	1-85937-427-1	£9.99
Southport (pb)	1-85937-425-5	£9.99
Staffordshire	1-85937-047-0	£12.99
Stratford upon Avon	1-85937-098-5	£12.99
Suffolk (pb)	1-85937-221-x	£9.99
Suffolk Coast	1-85937-259-7	£14.99
Surrey (pb)	1-85937-240-6	£9.99
Sussex (pb)	1-85937-184-1	£9.99
Swansea (pb)	1-85937-167-1	£9.99
Tees Valley & Cleveland	1-85937-211-2	£14.99
Thanet (pb)	1-85937-116-7	£9.99
Tiverton (pb)	1-85937-178-7	£9.99
Torbay	1-85937-063-2	£12.99
Truro	1-85937-147-7	£12.99
Victorian and Edwardian Cornwall	1-85937-252-x	£14.99
Victorian & Edwardian Devon	1-85937-253-8	£14.99
Victorian & Edwardian Kent	1-85937-149-3	£14.99
Vic & Ed Maritime Album	1-85937-144-2	£17.99
Victorian and Edwardian Sussex	1-85937-157-4	£14.99
Victorian & Edwardian Yorkshire	1-85937-154-x	£14.99
Victorian Seaside	1-85937-159-0	£17.99
Villages of Devon (pb)	1-85937-293-7	£9.99
Villages of Kent (pb)	1-85937-294-5	£9.99
Villages of Sussex (pb)	1-85937-295-3	£9.99
Warwickshire (pb)	1-85937-203-1	£9.99
Welsh Castles (pb)	1-85937-322-4	£9.99
West Midlands (pb)	1-85937-289-9	£9.99
West Sussex	1-85937-148-5	£14.99
West Yorkshire (pb)	1-85937-201-5	£9.99
Weymouth (pb)	1-85937-209-0	£9.99
Wiltshire (pb)	1-85937-277-5	£9.99
Wiltshire Churches (pb)	1-85937-171-x	£9.99
Wiltshire Living Memories	1-85937-245-7	£14.99
Winchester (pb)	1-85937-428-x	£9.99
Windmills & Watermills	1-85937-242-2	£17.99
Worcester (pb)	1-85937-165-5	£9.99
Worcestershire	1-85937-152-3	£14.99
York (pb)	1-85937-199-x	£9.99
Yorkshire (pb)	1-85937-186-8	£9.99
Yorkshire Living Memories	1-85937-166-3	£14.99

See Frith books on the internet www.francisfrith.co.uk

FRITH PRODUCTS & SERVICES

Francis Frith would doubtless be pleased to know that the pioneering publishing venture he started in 1860 still continues today. A hundred and forty years later, The Francis Frith Collection continues in the same innovative tradition and is now one of the foremost publishers of vintage photographs in the world. Some of the current activities include:

Interior Decoration

Today Frith's photographs can be seen framed and as giant wall murals in thousands of pubs, restaurants, hotels, banks, retail stores and other public buildings throughout the country. In every case they enhance the unique local atmosphere of the places they depict and provide reminders of gentler days in an increasingly busy and frenetic world.

Product Promotions

Frith products are used by many major companies to promote the sales of their own products or to reinforce their own history and heritage. Frith promotions have been used by Hovis bread, Courage beers, Scots Porage Oats, Colman's mustard, Cadbury's foods, Mellow Birds coffee, Dunhill pipe tobacco, Guinness, and Bulmer's Cider.

Genealogy and Family History

As the interest in family history and roots grows world-wide, more and more people are turning to Frith's photographs of Great Britain for images of the towns, villages and streets where their ancestors lived; and, of course, photographs of the churches and chapels where their ancestors were christened, married and buried are an essential part of every genealogy tree and family album.

Frith Products

All Frith photographs are available Framed or just as Mounted Prints and Posters (size 23 x 16 inches). These may be ordered from the address below. From time to time other products - Address Books, Calendars, Table Mats, etc - are available.

The Internet

Already twenty thousand Frith photographs can be viewed and purchased on the internet through the Frith websites and a myriad of partner sites.

For more detailed information on Frith companies and products, look at these sites:

www.francisfrith.co.uk
www.francisfrith.com
(for North American visitors)

See the complete list of Frith Books at:

www.francisfrith.co.uk

This web site is regularly updated with the latest list of publications from the Frith Book Company. If you wish to buy books relating to another part of the country that your local bookshop does not stock, you may purchase on-line.

For further information, trade, or author enquiries please contact us at the address below:

The Francis Frith Collection, Frith's Barn, Teffont, Salisbury, Wiltshire, England SP3 5QP.
Tel: +44 (0)1722 716 376 Fax: +44 (0)1722 716 881 Email: sales@francisfrith.co.uk

See Frith books on the internet www.francisfrith.co.uk

TO RECEIVE YOUR FREE MOUNTED PRINT

Mounted Print
Overall size 14 x 11 inches

Cut out this Voucher and return it with your remittance for £1.95 to cover postage and handling, to UK addresses. For overseas addresses please include £4.00 post and handling. Choose any photograph included in this book. Your SEPIA print will be A4 in size, and mounted in a cream mount with burgundy rule line, overall size 14 x 11 inches.

Order additional Mounted Prints at HALF PRICE (only £7.49 each*)
If there are further pictures you would like to order, possibly as gifts for friends and family, purchase them at half price (no additional postage and handling required).

Have your Mounted Prints framed*
For an additional £14.95 per print you can have your chosen Mounted Print framed in an elegant polished wood and gilt moulding, overall size 16 x 13 inches (no additional postage and handling required).

*** IMPORTANT!**
These special prices are only available if ordered using the original voucher on this page (no copies permitted) and at the same time as your free Mounted Print, for delivery to the same address

Frith Collectors' Guild

From time to time we publish a magazine of news and stories about Frith photographs and further special offers of Frith products. If you would like 12 months FREE membership, please return this form.

Send completed forms to:
The Francis Frith Collection, Frith's Barn, Teffont, Salisbury, Wiltshire SP3 5QP

Voucher for FREE and Reduced Price Frith Prints

Picture no.	Page number	Qty	Mounted @ £7.49	Framed + £14.95	Total Cost
		1	**Free of charge***	£	£
			£7.49	£	£
			£7.49	£	£
			£7.49	£	£
			£7.49	£	£
			£7.49	£	£

Please allow 28 days for delivery — *** Post & handling** — **£1.95**

Book Title .... **Total Order Cost** **£**

Please do not photocopy this voucher. Only the original is valid, so please cut it out and return it to us.

I enclose a cheque / postal order for £ ....
made payable to 'The Francis Frith Collection'
OR please debit my Mastercard / Visa / Switch / Amex card
(credit cards please on all overseas orders)

Number ....

Issue No (Switch only) .... Valid from (Amex/Switch) ....

Expires .... Signature ....

Name Mr/Mrs/Ms ....

Address ....

....

....

.... Postcode ....

Daytime Tel No ....

Valid to 31/12/02

The Francis Frith Collectors' Guild

Please enrol me as a member for 12 months free of charge.

Name Mr/Mrs/Ms ....

Address ....

....

....

.... Postcode ....

Free Print - see overleaf

Would you like to find out more about Francis Frith?

We have recently recruited some entertaining speakers who are happy to visit local groups, clubs and societies to give an illustrated talk documenting Frith's travels and photographs. If you are a member of such a group and are interested in hosting a presentation, we would love to hear from you.

Our speakers bring with them a small selection of our local town and county books, together with sample prints. They are happy to take orders. A small proportion of the order value is donated to the group who have hosted the presentation. The talks are therefore an excellent way of fundraising for small groups and societies.

Can you help us with information about any of the Frith photographs in this book?

We are gradually compiling an historical record for each of the photographs in the Frith archive. It is always fascinating to find out the names of the people shown in the pictures, as well as insights into the shops, buildings and other features depicted.

If you recognize anyone in the photographs in this book, or if you have information not already included in the author's caption, do let us know. We would love to hear from you, and will try to publish it in future books or articles.

Our production team

Frith books are produced by a small dedicated team at offices in the converted Grade II listed 18th-century barn at Teffont near Salisbury, illustrated above. Most have worked with the Frith Collection for many years. All have in common one quality: they have a passion for the Frith Collection. The team is constantly expanding, but currently includes:

Jason Buck, John Buck, Douglas Burns, Heather Crisp, Isobel Hall, Rob Hames, Hazel Heaton, Peter Horne, James Kinnear, Tina Leary, Hannah Marsh, Eliza Sackett, Terence Sackett, Sandra Sanger, Shelley Tolcher, Susanna Walker, Clive Wathen and Jenny Wathen.